COOKING
WITHOUT FUSS

COOKING
WITHOUT FUSS

stress-free recipes for the homecook

JONNY HAUGHTON

photography by Myles Nelson

PAVILION

For my darling Cam

First published in the United Kingdom in 2005
by PAVILION BOOKS

An imprint of **Chrysalis** Books Group plc

The Chrysalis Building, Bramley Road, London W10 6SP
www.chrysalisbooks.co.uk

A CIP catalogue record for this book is available from the British Library.

ISBN 1 86205 699 4

ASSOCIATE PUBLISHER: Kate Oldfield
SENIOR EDITOR: Lizzy Gray
DESIGN: Adelle Morris & Gemma Wilson

Reproduction by Classicscan, Singapore
Printed in Singapore

10 9 8 7 6 5 4 3 2 1

The author would welcome your feedback. If you have any comments about the recipes, please feel free to email him at jonnyhaughton2@tiscali.com.

CONTENTS

Foreword by Simon Hopkinson   6

Introduction   7

Author's Notes, Tips and General Advice   10

Here Comes the Sun   **20**

Light Bites and Salads   22

Grills   41

Curries   61

Summer Desserts   72

In From the Cold   **82**

Soups   84

Starters and Lunch Dishes   95

Stews and Other Hearty Fare   113

Winter Puddings   134

Side Dishes and Basic Recipes   146

Recommended Suppliers   156

Index   158

Acknowledgements   160

FOREWORD
by Simon Hopkinson

I have praised Jonny Haughton's food at The Havelock Tavern in the past and now, in this long-awaited book, I have the opportunity to do so again.

I have eaten some really good food in my time but, not to put too finer point on it, some of Jonny's food I have eaten has been as good as that which I have eaten anywhere. Ever.

It is of a quality I had thought was on the decline. It is always served without fuss and with pride and charm. Luckily this food is available to me after a brisk two-minute walk from my front door, in the more undulating borders of Shepherd's Bush and Brook Green in West London. However his food is not "London" food nor simply good gastropub food. It is great food that could and should be enjoyed anywhere.

You might think you have seen these sort of dishes everywhere, recently. But then, everyone copies everyone at some time. Here however, they taste as if each recipe has been devised last week.

It is high time that Jonny's intelligent ideas, economics and traditional cooking principles were conveyed to all. So, whether you are a novice or an experienced cook, I hope you enjoy Jonny's recipes as much as I do.

INTRODUCTION

The recipes in this book are some of the most popular from The Havelock Tavern in London's Brook Green. If you haven't been, it's the type of place anyone can eat, drink and feel at home in. A good, honest pub with, above all, delicious food. It's not particularly sophisticated but then our kitchen is pretty small, which limits what we can do. Indeed, this is one of the reasons why I think our food is suitable for the home-cook – our kitchen is probably no bigger than yours! The cooking we like to do is what the French would call "bonne bouffe" – good, unpretentious cookery – the sort of food all of us would do well to eat more of.

Not only has it been my workplace for the last ten years or so, it's also been home to my wife Camilla and our family. Living above the shop has its moments. There is little privacy, for instance, when you need it. But it has proved to be a marvellous place to bring up our three children, Georgia, Gus and Max. They have benefited from the vibrant, social atmosphere – it's almost a community within a community. And I derive tremendous pleasure from the way they are developing a natural, and hopefully lasting, interest in food. Being exposed to fantastic and unusual ingredients is bound to be stimulating.

Since I started cooking professionally, I have reached the conclusion that eating out – and eating in – is nothing to do with the price of the ingredients, it's the way they are treated that counts. In other words, whether it is a piece of foie gras or a cabbage, both require the same care and attention. I also began to realize that cooking with a degree of thriftiness can be highly pleasurable: not only are the cheaper cuts usually the most flavoursome but also being careful with ingredients can sometimes lead to moments of inspired creativity. "Necessity being the mother of invention" has become our watchword in the kitchen and underpins everything we do.

I will always find a way of using up something one way or another. If this sounds rather worthy – try it, it's rather satisfying making something out of nothing!

My aim at The Havelock has always been to put interesting and nutritious food on the plate – and to achieve consistency, that most elusive of qualities. We change our menu twice a day. This may seem like an exercise in masochism but it's more fun and to me seems a natural way to cook. If it's a little precarious sometimes, we have learnt to improvise. If something isn't available or we forget to order a product, we use something else. As long as it is fresh and a high quality, nothing else matters. When it comes to eating, the question of taste should override all other considerations. And attention to detail is vital. So, it's important to get the simple things right, whether it is a bowl of chips or bread. I can say I get as much pleasure from cooking these straightforward things well as I do from our more ambitious efforts.

Firstly, you will find useful tips with notes on ingredients and menu planning. There is also basic advice on kitchen equipment and how to deal with catering for large numbers. "Here comes the Sun" is a collection of dishes featuring

grills, salads and curries – suitable for those summer days when all you want to eat is something light. "In from the Cold" contains many of our favourite rustic soups and stews – as well as terrific one-pot dishes that save time and can be relied upon to produce superb results. Consider the sight and aroma of a whole shoulder of lamb that has been braising in the oven for seven hours – wafts of garlic, rosemary and white wine assailing you as you lift the lid. What could be more effortless and yet as delectable? All you have to do is throw it in the oven and wait. A bit of mash, a few green beans and, voilà, a beautiful meal made simple. Both parts contain chapters on puddings, which are designed to make the most of their respective seasons.

I know, having bought countless cookbooks for myself, you may just flick through these pages and admire the photographs – that is great, but I can promise you, you will achieve excellent results from this book. If you enjoy cooking and eating as I do, you will get real pleasure from producing the sort of simple food everyone loves to eat.

Jonny Haughton

AUTHOR'S NOTES, TIPS AND GENERAL ADVICE

Seasoning

No area is quite as problematic as seasoning for the food writer: what is salty to one person is bland to another. There is also the concern about too much salt in the modern diet – to my mind, a proven one. Still, this is not a book about how to lead a healthier life – it's about how to cook food that tastes better. Whether you like it or not, salt in all its guises is the number one flavour enhancer. I have decided, therefore, to leave the degree of seasoning to your taste.

All I would say is that professional chefs – in good kitchens at least – are taught to season boldly. Novice chefs in my kitchen are always amazed at how much salt is required to season food properly. This essential skill is not as easy as you might think and can take a bit of time to master. It involves constant tasting and adjusting – and also trying to imagine how the food will taste in three or four mouthfuls' time. In my experience, this is one of the fundamental differences between restaurant and home cooking.

Stocks

Probably nothing is more important to the professional than having good-quality stock. I realize few people have the time or inclination to make stock of their own. It's a pity but that's life. So, what are the options?

shop-bought stocks: probably the best option but shop-bought versions can be weak. One way round this, admittedly expensive, is to buy double the amount you need for the recipe. Bring it to the boil in a saucepan and reduce it by half to concentrate its flavour. Try Daylesford's Organic Chicken Stock, Joubere's Fish Stock or Donald Russell's Lamb and Beef Stock.

stock cubes: full of salt and E numbers – some brands contain monosodium glutamate (MSG). Stick to the vegetable versions. Decent brands are Marigold Organic and Telma. Consider using Star Porcini Stock Cubes – the Italian housewife's favourite, apparently.

bottled concentrated bouillons: again, these can contain MSG and too much salt. Try Knorr's Touch of Taste Chicken.

stock concentrates: not a bad option, these are available from most supermarkets. Another option is to buy in bulk from the internet. Divide up into small quantities and freeze.

CONVERSION TABLES

All these are approximate conversions, which have either been rounded up or down. All spoon measurements in this book are level, unless specified otherwise.

Weights		Dimensions	
₂oz	10g	⅛ inch	3mm
¼	20	¼	5mm
	25	½	1cm
½	40	¾	2
	50	1	2.5
½	60	1¼	3
	75	1½	4
	110	1¾	4.5
4½	125	2	5
5	150	2½	6
6	175	3	7.5
	200	3½	9
	225	4	10
	250	5	13
0	275	5¼	13.5
2	350	6	15
lb	450	6½	16
lb 8oz	700	7	18
	900	7½	19
	1.35kg	8	20
		9	23
		9½	24
		10	25.5
		11	28
		12	30

Basic ingredients

I thought it would be good to define some of the basic ingredients used in the book. Unless otherwise specified:

- Butter is unsalted
- Vegetable oil is groundnut or sunflower
- Eggs are medium
- Olive oil is pure, as opposed to extra virgin
- Salt is table salt as opposed to sea salt
- A large onion is about 225g; a small onion is 100g
- Tomato purée is purée, not concentrate
- Bacon is whole, unsmoked streaky
- Herbs are fresh

Portion sizes

This is a tricky one. Appetites vary and you'll be needing plenty for "seconds". Here are a few ground rules to help you decide:

Fish: allow 225g of boneless, skinless fish per portion. If you are buying whole fish, allow 450g per portion. The exceptions are monkfish and skate, which are generally sold headless but not boneless: allow 340g per portion. Larger fish are more expensive than portion size fish. The upside is you get a slightly better yield and the fillets are thicker. For shellfish, allow about 350g per serving.

Meat: basically the same as fish. Allow 225g of boneless meat per portion. Buying meat on the bone, for example forerib of beef, allow 360g per portion.

Cooking terminology

I have tried to avoid the use of professional cooking terminology and I apologize if the odd, unintelligible expression crops up. For the sake of clarity, here are some of the most commonly used expressions:

Boil means cooking uncovered over a high heat: vigorous bubbling is apparent.

Chop (as in onions) means cutting into dice.

Volume	
fl oz	55ml
	75
5 (¼ pint)	150
0 (½ pint)	275
pint	570
¼	725
¾	1litre
	1.2
½	1.5
	2.25

Oven temperatures		
Gas mark 1	275°F	140°C
2	300	150
3	325	170
4	350	180
5	375	190
6	400	200
7	425	220
8	450	230
9	475	240

Liquids		
American	Imperial	ml/litres
tsp	1 tsp	5ml
fl oz	1 tbsp	15ml
¼ cup	4 tbsp	55ml
½ cup plus 2 tbsp	¼ pint	150ml
¼ cups	½ pint	275ml
pint/16fl oz	¾ pint	450ml
2½ pints		
5 cups	2 pints	1.2 litres
0 pints	8 pints	4.8 litres

Slice means cutting into thin slivers.

Poach means cooking covered at simmering point.

Simmer means cooking uncovered, just below boiling point. The odd bubble should be coming to the surface.

Stewing (as in vegetables) means cooking in oil or butter, covered, over a very low heat, stirring from time to time to avoid the ingredients sticking to the bottom of the pan.

Some of the recipes call for **cooked green vegetables** such as green beans, broad beans and spinach. These need to be cooked until al dente and then refreshed. This means cooking them and immediately plunging them straight into cold water to stop the cooking process. Once cool, they need to be really well drained in a colander before further use.

Dry-roasting refers to the Indian technique of cooking whole spices prior to grinding. This is to bring out their full aromatic qualities. Put the spices in a heavy-bottomed frying pan (no need to use oil) and over a moderate to high heat, fry the spices until they start to produce an aromatic smell. One way of telling when they are ready is the seeds will start to pop and dance about in the pan. You are not aiming to colour the spices. Should you find that you have overcooked them, throw them away and start again.

Baking blind refers to covering a pastry case (prior to baking) with foil or greaseproof paper and weighing it down with "baking beans" – we use dried chickpeas. The purpose is to stop the pastry from rising – this results in a crisper, more compact pastry. Normally, the tart case is cooked for 10–15 minutes with the baking beans. They are then removed and the tart is returned to the oven for a further 5–10 minutes in order to colour the pastry to a light, golden brown.

Grated garlic is an expression used throughout the book. This is my preferred method of crushing garlic. I use either an ordinary box grater or, more usually, a microplane. It's a personal habit possibly borne out of laziness. Using a garlic crusher, the back of a knife or a pestle and mortar are the more conventional methods – they all achieve the same result.

Professional cooking tips

I shouldn't really be giving out all the tricks of the trade. But actually the secret of cooking well is very simple: it's all about attention to detail. So at the risk of telling you something you already know, here are a few pointers, which are sensible, common practice in most professional kitchens:

Dried pulses should be cooked in large volumes of unsalted water. Ideally soak them for 48 hours before cooking. Do not season pulses until they are completely tender. It is perfectly fine to add a sprinkling of bicarbonate of soda to their soaking and cooking water – this helps to soften the pulses. Most of the recipes specify "canned" pulses – these should always be rinsed prior to use.

Fish is best cooked on the bone. It's tastier and more succulent. If you are frying fish, dredge in a mix of flour and semolina flour seasoned with salt and pepper. This provides a very thin batter that gives the fish a crisp coating and helps it to stay moist.

Buying fish is a matter of using common sense. If the fish smells of fish, avoid it. Really fresh fish actually smells of very little. I think the best physical test is the gills. If they are a dull red, the fish is old – they should be bright red. It also helps to know what fish are in season – it's always preferable to cook with locally caught fish from day boats. Farmed fish is more problematic. Freshness is less of an issue but the question of quality is difficult particularly when you can't be sure what constitutes their diet. There is a general concern about the texture of farmed fish – salmon in particular can be flabby. With wild salmon two or three times the price, "you pays your money and makes your choice".

Garlic can vary in quality and size. Old garlic is stronger than fresh and should be used more sparingly. The way you prepare garlic will affect its pungency: the less you do to it, the milder it is. Crushing or puréeing produces harsh and fiery notes. Always peel and use at the last moment. Never buy processed garlic, dried, frozen, in tubes or otherwise.

Green vegetables should be cooked in large volumes of heavily salted water. This is to cook them as quickly as possible in order to retain their colour and nutrients. The water should be almost as salty as sea water.

Celery should always be peeled prior to use. This is a small but important detail. The purpose is to remove the stringy bits which, while not inedible, are annoying to eat.

Herbs, fresh and dried, are invaluable. Treat them carefully. Dried herbs are generally stronger than fresh. Oregano, herbes de Provence, tarragon, bay leaves are all good. Avoid dried sage, parsley and basil. Whatever dried herbs you have in your cupboard, throw them out once a year and replenish.

To prolong the life of fresh herbs, refrigerate them in sealed plastic bags – they last a surprisingly long time. In general, soft herbs should be added towards the end of cooking; hard herbs such as rosemary, sage and thyme at the beginning.

Onions are so important in most of what we eat. Prepare them carefully. Never peel an onion until you are ready to start cooking with it. Peel the onion completely – tough, outer onion leaves can never be made tender by any amount of cooking.

Chop onions as finely as you can – this simple step will do more to improve your cooking than anything else.

Pepper should be a 50:50 combination of black and white: the first for flavour, the second for heat. Fill your grinder up with a combination of both. Pink peppercorns should be steered clear of.

Roasts should always be brought to room temperature before cooking – allow a couple of hours. Rest a large joint in a warm place for at least 25 minutes before carving. This gives the fibres a chance to relax and produces a more succulent piece of meat.

Roast tomatoes (see recipe on page 152), though ubiquitous, are actually useful things to have around. In most recipes, you can usually substitute "fried" tomatoes. Do not be tempted to use sun-dried tomatoes or sunblush tomatoes – I find the latter are delicious, if a little intense. To fry the tomatoes, chop them up, season generously with salt and pepper and stew in a little butter or olive oil until they start to collapse – usually about 10 minutes. If you want a more refined product, skin the tomatoes first by plunging them into boiling water for 10–15 seconds.

For **roast peppers**, preheat a heavy-bottomed frying pan or ridged grill pan (I quite often stick them on that really hot heat you get from a barbecue prior to the coals going grey). You could also use an overhead grill though it's more of a fiddle to see what's going on. Chop off any stalks and rub a little vegetable oil over the peppers. Place on to the grill and turn over until all sides are blistered and blackened. Pop into a plastic bag and leave to cool. Scrape off the skin, then slice it in two and remove the seeds.

Shellfish preparation is pretty simple. The golden rule is to discard any that are broken or that do not close when tapped. If in doubt, chuck.

Mussels may need "debearding" before cooking. This involves using your thumb and forefinger to pull off the bits of weed that are still attached to the mollusc. I don't worry about the barnacles, but do scrape them off if you can be bothered. All shellfish should be washed. Actually what they don't like is to sit in ordinary tap water – eventually they will die (mussels are surprisingly robust little things – think of them clinging to sun-baked rocks at low tide). The best way to wash mussels is to put them in a large and roomy colander – give them a light shake – and pour plenty of cold water over them. Keep them refrigerated until needed. Avoid putting them in sealed containers – just cover them with a damp piece of kitchen paper.

The correct way to clean **clams** is to put them in a single layer in a shallow tray of salted water (not quite covering them) and leave them in peace. Sea water is ideal but diluting salt in tap water works just as well. After ten minutes or so (when they think no-one is looking) they become very active and start squirting water, including sand and grit, all over the place. Leave them at it for a couple of hours while you contemplate what to do with them. Rinse and they are ready for use. Again, store in the fridge covered with a damp piece of kitchen paper. This method works with **cockles** too.

Spices should be bought whole and ground finely to order. Invest in a small electric coffee grinder (or you can use a pestle and mortar, if you feel like a little upper arm exercise). Purge your spice rack at least once a year. Throw the whole lot in the bin and start again.

Stews and tomato-based sauces improve as they mature. Try and cook them at least a day in advance. When making a stew, take care to brown the meat. This is an essential first step. One of our favourite sayings in the kitchen is "colour is flavour!" (there is usually a chorus of this when somebody burns something). And it's true –

after salt, it's probably the easiest way of enhancing the flavour of something (think of undercooked bacon). Fry the meat in small batches to avoid overcrowding the pan. Adding a little butter helps the browning process.

Classic **stew-making** dictates you toss the meat in seasoned flour before frying. I am not convinced by this. Firstly, you end up colouring the flour rather than the meat. Secondly, the flour (and seasoning) is going to dissolve during the cooking process. To me, it makes more sense neither to flour nor season the meat before frying it. It's better to season the stew at the beginning and make final adjustments at the end. Thicken the stew by sprinkling the cooked vegetables with flour. Then add your cooking liquid (wine, stock, etc) before returning the browned meat to the pan.

Choosing a menu

Choosing the right dishes for a meal is about balance. Hopefully you know your guests and what will please them.

At The Havelock, we have been changing our menu twice a day for the past ten years. When we are deciding what to put on the menu, there are certain givens: a general adherence to the seasons; an understanding that, for whatever reason, people tend to eat more lightly at lunchtime; and that the food can be properly executed given the resources available on the day. We also take great care to ensure that there are enough dishes to appeal to both sexes. Speaking for myself, men are less bothered about their carb intake although times are changing – you'd be amazed by how many women order side chips!

The golden rule is to avoid repetition. After all, you are seeking to produce a harmonious meal that stimulates the senses and provides interest as each course arrives. The best way to ensure this is to provide variety and contrast. Consider a hot starter if you are having a cold main course. If you are cooking a meaty main course, plan a vegetable or fish starter. If your main course is robust, opt for a light appetizer such as a salad or serve a few canapés instead. If one of the dishes uses a lot of cream, for example, avoid it elsewhere. Vary the cooking methods so if you are having something grilled to start with, aim for something stewed or poached later on. Above all, avoid the repetitive use of ingredients.

Cooking for crowds

For many people, catering for large numbers can be an ordeal. At least the homecook has the advantage of knowing exactly how many people to feed. In the professional world, order can turn to chaos in the blink of an eye. people can turn up out of nowhere! And so professional chefs learn to be flexible, always ready for the worst-case scenario. Preparation and organization are the watchwords for feeding large numbers successfully at home.

Even then, danger is lurking round every corner. I was once asked to cover a shift for a friend who – how can I put it? – landed me in it. It was a Saturday night and not only was the restaurant full but there was a stag night for 50 people in the function room as well. I was feeling tired and my wife was expecting our second baby. To cut a long story short, 40 of the 50 stags had the chicken, a dish I had never cooked before.

Shortly after serving the food, one of the chickens was sent back for further cooking. Followed a few moments later by another. Then another until all 40 plates were returned with half-eaten food. I didn't know what to do. It was impossible to tell whose food was whose and while this was going on, the regular diners needed to be fed. It was one of those horrible, sinking moments. In the end, we managed to sort something out (including a large discount) and I walked into the night chastened and a little wiser. Many years later, I met somebody who started telling me about this appalling experience they had suffered on a stag night in a restaurant we both knew. Needless to say, I kept my mouth shut.

The moral of this story is two-fold: if you are feeling tired, do not over-extend yourself. Play it safe. Much better to produce an ordinary dish well than an ambitious one badly. Or get in caterers. Secondly, do not risk poisoning your friends – they will never forget it.

Here are a few practical pointers to avoid the most common pitfalls of mass catering:
- Do not produce anything that requires any last-minute timing.
- Do not produce anything that prevents you from being a good host, such as by being tied to a barbecue.

- Avoid anything for which you do not have sufficient refrigeration.
- Avoid anything that requires last-minute slicing or opening, such as oysters.
- Choose dishes that do not deteriorate easily, such as soups, stews, curries, tarts, charcuterie and so on.

A quick guide to essential kitchen equipment

Professional chefs have the advantage of working with the right equipment for the job. Here is a list of what I would consider essential kitchen equipment (for suppliers, see page 156):

Baking sheets should be the width of your oven and heavy duty, so that they do not buckle.

Chopping boards should be large and heavy (at least 60 x 40cm). I would always use a plastic board over a wooden one. You need two of them. A good tip is to place a damp cloth under your board. This helps keep it secure while you chop.

Colanders: you need a large (40cm) and a small (26cm).

Frying pans should be ovenproof, heavy-bottomed and made of iron. You need a small omelette pan (20cm), a medium pan (26cm) and a large one (32cm). Keep oiled and avoid the use of metal scourers.

Gratin dishes should be heavy and made of enamelled cast-iron. Le Creuset is the best brand and will last a lifetime.

Knives that are lightweight and cheap should be thrown away. Get rid of them and free up some space. Invest in three knives. You need a

chopping knife (23cm blade); a paring knife (10cm blade) and a carving knife (26cm blade). Invest in decent varieties – the diamond-tipped ones are the best.

So many people have a drawer full of blunt knives. Not only are they a danger (you have to exert more pressure) but they also take some of the pleasure out of food preparation. Invest in one of those magnetic knife strips that you mount on the wall – quite expensive but they will help keep your knives sharp.

Loose metal tart rings to fit on your baking tray: get two (23cm and 26cm).

Mandolin for slicing: buy the French stainless steel ones – admittedly more expensive, but aesthetically pleasing nonetheless.

Metal bowls are indispensable. They should have a diameter of at least 26cm and should be made of stainless steel. Buy a minimum of three.

A mouli-legumes is essential for purées and mash.

Roasting trays should be at the least the width of your oven. A good roasting tray needs to be heavy-bottomed with handles – a tray full of hot fat that buckles is a dangerous thing.

Rubber spatulas are probably the single most useful thing in the kitchen. Essential for scraping out bowls, for folding and for stirring – you can now get heat-resistant ones.

Saucepans should be ovenproof (no plastic handles or knobs), heavy-bottomed and made of steel. A good pan will last a lifetime and is money well-spent. Bourgeat is the first choice for most professional chefs.

Spring-form cake tins come in various sizes. Aim for non-stick versions. You will need at least one 23cm tin.

And don't forget, you will need a variety of smaller utensils such as:

• Fine sieve
• Fish slice
• Large metal spoons, including slotted metal spoons
• Tongs

HERE COMES THE SUN

When it comes to food, summer is definitely a case of less is more. Whether it is a picnic in the country or a barbecue on the beach, what you are after is light and clean-tasting food. Now is the time to be eating fish, ideally grilled with simple accompaniments – the Marinated Lemon and Fennel Salad, for instance, goes brilliantly with any oily fish such as mackerel and sea trout.

Warm weather also demands colourful salads with loads of vibrant vegetables. I always think aromatic curries come into their own and are perfect for feeding large numbers. It's also the best time of year for stoned fruit and berries – remind yourself what a great combination Peaches and Cream are or try the Brown Sugar Meringue With Strawberries and Orange. Whatever your favourite ingredients, think light and keep it simple.

LIGHT BITES
AND SALADS

We know a bit about tarts here at The Havelock. We have served one on our lunch menu everyday for the past ten years, usually vegetarian. The key to this recipe is the custard: this ratio of cream and egg yolks produces a rich, harmonious texture, which you can use to achieve endless variations with different vegetables and cheese.

Sweet Onion and Parmesan Tart

SERVES 8

25g butter

6 large onions, thinly sliced

1 garlic clove, finely sliced

1tbsp chopped thyme

Salt and pepper

1 quantity Savoury Pastry (see page 155)

Flour for dusting

6 egg yolks

425ml double cream

125g Parmesan cheese, grated

In a roomy, heavy-bottomed saucepan, melt the butter. When hot, add the onions, garlic and thyme and season generously with salt and pepper. Let the onions stew for at least 45 minutes so that they become soft and slippery. You will need to keep a watchful eye as you do not want the onions to colour.

Thinly roll out the pastry on a lightly floured board using a floured rolling pin; use to line a 28-cm tart ring, leaving a 1-cm overhang. Leave to rest for 30 minutes in the fridge. Meanwhile, preheat the oven to 190°C/375°F/Gas Mark 5. Blind bake the tart case (see page 12) for 10 minutes. Remove the baking beans and paper and return the tart case to the oven for a further 10–15 minutes, or until lightly golden brown. Put the tart case aside.

Tip the onions into a colander suspended over a bowl. Lightly press the onions to encourage the juices to flow. (Keep these juices for your next soup or stock-making session.) You can complete this stage up to 3 days ahead.

In a bowl, mix the egg yolks, cream and Parmesan. Add the onions and give the mix a good stir. Taste and adjust the seasoning if necessary – it will certainly need more salt but be careful because of the Parmesan. Pour the onion mixture into the tart case and smooth the surface.

Return the tart case to the oven and bake for 20 minutes, or until golden brown (the timing will depend on how hot your onions are). Trim off the pastry overhang and slide the tart on to a serving dish. Leave to cool for 10 minutes before serving.

These are a shallow-fried version of falafel, found everywhere throughout the Middle East. Serve with a salad of Cos lettuce, tomatoes, cucumber, flat-leaf parsley and mint. They are light and very good.

Spiced Chickpea Fritters with Sesame Dressing

SERVES 4

500g canned chickpeas, drained weight, rinsed

2tsp cumin seeds

2tsp coriander seeds

1 red onion, finely chopped

2tbsp finely chopped parsley

1tbsp finely chopped coriander

½ red chilli, deseeded and finely chopped

1 garlic clove, puréed

1 tsp tahini paste (optional)

1 egg

Salt and pepper

2–3tbsp seasoned plain white flour

Vegetable oil for frying

For the sesame dressing

100ml Greek yoghurt

3tbsp milk

½ garlic clove, grated

1tbsp sesame oil

Put the chickpeas in a clean tea towel and give them a gentle squeeze to remove any excess moisture. (This step is vital otherwise the mix will be wet and will not hold together.) Put them into the bowl of a food processor and chop until they resemble coarse breadcrumbs – in other words, do not overprocess.

Lightly toast the spices in a dry pan, then grind finely. Add the spices to the chickpeas, together with the remaining ingredients and season generously with salt and pepper. Blend briefly to combine.

Roll the chickpea mixture into balls the size of a large plum, flatten slightly into patties and dredge through a tray of seasoned flour, shaking off the excess. At this stage, it is not a bad idea to refrigerate them for 30 minutes to allow them to firm up.

When you are ready to eat, heat a thin layer of vegetable oil in a large frying pan until it shimmers. Add the fritters and fry for about 5 minutes in total, until golden brown on both sides. Drain briefly on kitchen paper before serving. Fry the fritters in batches, if necessary, to avoid overcrowding the pan and keep warm in a low oven until they are all fried.

To make the dressing, whisk all the ingredients together and season with salt and pepper to taste. Serve the fritters warm with the sauce on the side.

Making a proper tortilla is a real art form. The trick is to use a **non-stick** heavy-bottomed frying pan and to caramelize the onions. Unless you like things really spicy, buy the mild "dulce" version of chorizo, not the "picante". Serve with a salad of green beans and rocket. You will need a 26-cm frying pan.

Potato Tortilla with Chorizo in Red Wine

SERVES 8

40g butter

6 onions, very finely sliced

2 garlic cloves, finely sliced

8 eggs

8 new potatoes, cooked, peeled and finely sliced

Salt and pepper

750g fresh chorizo sausage, thickly sliced

2 bay leaves, torn into pieces

350ml red wine, such as Rioja

In a large and roomy saucepan, melt 20g of the butter and add the onions and garlic. Over a brisk heat, fry the onions – stirring as necessary – until they develop a rich, golden colour. Be watchful as the onions start to caramelize – you will need to stir more frequently in the latter stages. The process will take at least half an hour if not longer. There should be no excess liquid, so drain if necessary. Note the lack of seasoning.

Preheat the grill to high.

In a large bowl, beat the eggs, add the cooked onions and potatoes and season generously with salt and pepper (it needs to be well seasoned).

Melt the remaining butter in the frying pan. When it is just beginning to foam, carefully add the tortilla mixture and smooth it out. Turn the heat down to low. Using a metal spatula, lift the tortilla from its edges and allow the runny egg to find its way underneath. Repeat this procedure every now and again until all the eggs are almost cooked.

Remove the pan from the heat and place under the hot grill for 1–2 minutes to finish the cooking. Put a serving plate (ideally round and flat) over the frying pan and invert the tortilla. Leave to cool slightly.

Meanwhile, put the chorizo into a saucepan that is just large enough to hold the sausages in a single layer. Add the bay leaves and cover with the wine. Bring to the boil, then turn down the heat and simmer gently for 25 minutes. Transfer the chorizo to a plate and reduce the wine by half.

Serve the tortilla warm with the thick slices of chorizo and a little of the red wine spooned over.

The salty creaminess of the feta goes terrifically well with the crisp, sweet vegetables. This is one of those salads that can be made in advance and is therefore handy for large gatherings. Soft goat's cheese can replace the feta. Unless you grow your own broad beans, shop-bought can be mealy: better to use frozen.

Broad Bean, Asparagus, Feta and Spiced Couscous Salad

SERVES 4

2 red onions, cut into 1-cm wedges

1tsp finely chopped thyme

1 garlic clove, finely sliced

4tbsp olive oil, plus extra for drizzling

Salt and pepper

50g couscous

½tsp ground cumin

½tsp ground coriander

Juice and zest of 1 lemon

½tsp ground, dried red chilli

½ garlic clove, grated

200g feta cheese, cut into 1-cm cubes

200g asparagus, cooked and cut into 3-cm slices

200g broad beans, cooked and peeled

2tbsp chopped mint

2tbsp chopped flat-leaf parsley

2tbsp extra virgin olive oil

1 small Cos lettuce

Preheat the oven to 220°C/425°F/Gas Mark 7.

Place a heavy-bottomed roasting tray in the oven to heat up. Put the onions, thyme and garlic into a bowl. Pour in a little olive oil, season with salt and pepper and toss thoroughly. Place the onions onto the hot tray and return to the oven. Check after 15 minutes and turn the onions if necessary. They will take 30 minutes in total.

Cook the couscous. Put in a bowl, season with salt and pepper and cover with boiling water. Stir with a fork to break up any lumps as they form. Leave to cool. Heat the olive oil in a small saucepan. When it is hot (not quite smoking point) add the spices, lemon zest (only), chilli and garlic, stir briefly, and immediately throw into the couscous. Add the red onions and mix.

To assemble the dish, place the feta and salad ingredients into a bowl. Add the lemon juice retained from the couscous. Stir in the couscous and serve in a large bowl on a bed of Cos lettuce leaves.

Everyone loves a Caesar salad – this is our version, which contains no anchovies. Add crispy bacon or grilled chicken for something more substantial. The recipe will make more dressing than you need, but it will keep well in the fridge for up to two weeks.

Salad of Cos Lettuce, Avocado, Buffalo Mozzarella and Parmesan Dressing

SERVES 4

1 large Cos lettuce, rinsed

2 ripe avocadoes, peeled, stoned and cut into chunks

250g buffalo mozzarella, torn into bite-sized pieces

2tbsp finely shredded basil

100g Roast Tomatoes (see page 152) or sunblushed tomatoes, peeled

2tbsp grated Parmesan cheese

Croûtons

4 slices of bread, medium-cut

2tbsp oilve oil

Pinch of thyme

1tsp crushed garlic

Salt and pepper

For the Parmesan dressing

2 egg yolks

4tbsp lemon juice

2tsp Dijon mustard

450ml vegetable oil

2 garlic cloves, crushed

75g Parmesan cheese, grated, plus extra for sprinkling

6tbsp water

Start by making the croûtons. Preheat the oven to 200°C/400°F/Gas Mark 6. Place the bread in a bowl and lightly toss together with the remaining ingredients. Tip on to a baking sheet and cook in the oven for 10–15 minutes. Give the croûtons a stir every 5 minutes. When golden brown, remove from the oven and leave to cool. Kept in a dry and airtight container, they will last for a week or so without going stale.

To make the dressing, place the egg yolks, lemon juice and mustard into a blender. Add a large pinch of salt and plenty of ground black pepper. With the motor running, gradually add the oil – drop by drop to start, then in a steady stream. Add the remaining ingredients and blend to the consistency of thick cream. Check the seasoning and add a little more salt if necessary. Cover and store in the fridge until you are ready to assemble the salad.

Place all the salad ingredients in a large bowl. Add enough dressing to coat the leaves, toss together and turn out into a serving bowl. Scatter the croûtons on top and sprinkle with more Parmesan.

This is a version of vitello tonnato using poached chicken instead of veal: it is terrifically good. It works well with cold roast chicken or pork, if you have any. The poaching method sounds a little improbable, but you'll end up with fantastically moist and flavoursome chicken. Serve with buttered new potatoes.

Salad of Poached Chicken, Green Beans, Watercress, Capers and Tuna Mayonnaise

SERVES 8

1 free-range chicken (1.5–2kg)

2 onions, finely chopped

2 garlic cloves

3 ribs of celery, finely chopped

3 small carrots, chopped

3 thyme sprigs

2 bay leaves

2 parsley sprigs

1tbsp black peppercorns

2 bunches of watercress, rinsed and spun

300g extra-fine green beans, topped and tailed, cooked and refreshed

For the tuna mayonnaise

2 egg yolks

300ml olive oil

Juice of 1½ lemons

3 canned anchovy fillets, finely chopped to a purée

100g canned tuna, drained, flaked

1½tbsp bottled or canned capers, rinsed or finely chopped

2tbsp chopped parsley

Salt and pepper

In a large and roomy pot, place the chicken, the vegetables and herbs and cover with cold water. Bring to the boil, then reduce the heat and simmer for 15 minutes. Remove the pot from the heat and leave the contents to cool in the liquid (still covered). When completely cold, remove the chicken from the pot and reduce the cooking liquid by half. Freeze for future use. Skin the chicken, then remove the flesh and cut it into bite-sized pieces. Put to one side.

Meanwhile, make the mayonnaise by using only half the oil and half the lemon juice (see page 153). Turn the mayonnaise into a bowl. Put the remaining oil and lemon juice into a food processor, together with the anchovies and tuna and blend until coarsely chopped. Fold this mixture into the mayonnaise. Add the chopped capers and parsley and adjust the seasoning with salt and plenty of pepper.

Fold the chicken into the mayonnaise to combine thoroughly and check the seasoning again. Arrange the watercress and green beans on a serving plate and pile the chicken mix on top.

There are many great ways to eat mussels: chorizo, bacon, tomato, chilli or garlic – all of these are fabulous combinations. The fresh thyme is what makes this version so good. Take care when cleaning mussels – discard any that do not close when tapped or are broken. See page 15 for further tips on cleaning and storing shellfish.

Steamed Mussels with Cider, Crème Fraîche and Thyme

SERVES 4

30g butter

1 large onion, finely sliced

2 garlic cloves, finely chopped

1tbsp finely chopped thyme

1.2kg mussels, debearded and rinsed

100ml medium cider

3tbsp crème fraîche

Pepper

In a heavy-bottomed and roomy pan, melt the butter and cook the onion, garlic and thyme for 10 minutes without colouring. Turn the heat up full, add the mussels and cider and cover with a tight-fitting lid. Steam the mussels until they are open, giving the pan a shake from time to time, about 5 minutes. Using a slotted spoon, remove the mussels to a large serving bowl. Add the crème fraîche to the mussel juices and boil over a high heat for a minute. Season with a little pepper and pour over the mussels. Serve with plenty of crusty bread to mop up the juices.

The key to this dish is to cook the squid quickly so that it is charred on the outside, tender and juicy within. Copious amounts of garlic and parsley bring it to life. A sturdy wok, if you have one, is the thing to cook this dish in.

Linguini with Squid, Red Chilli and Lemon

SERVES 4

100g linguini

Salt and pepper

300g squid tubes, thinly sliced into strips and wiped dry

Olive oil

3 garlic cloves, finely sliced

1 red chilli, deseeded and finely chopped

75ml dry white wine

4tbsp finely chopped flat-leaf parsley

2tbsp lemon juice

Make sure you have all the ingredients ready before you start. To cook the linguini, put a large pan of salted water on to boil. Add the linguini and boil until al dente.

Put a wok or large frying pan over a high heat and leave it there to get red hot. Put the squid into a bowl and lightly toss with salt, pepper and a little olive oil. (It is essential that the squid has been wiped dry beforehand.) Now, drop the squid into the wok – in batches to avoid overcrowding the pan – and stir-fry for no more than 1 minute.

Transfer the squid to a plate and continue stir-frying until all the squid is cooked. Turn the heat down to medium and fry the garlic and chilli for 1 minute. Add the white wine and boil hard to reduce by a half. Add the parsley, lemon juice and the cooked squid. Turn off the heat.

Drain the linguini well and tip it into the wok. Using a pair of tongs, toss the pasta and squid. Check the seasoning, add a little olive oil if it needs further lubrication and tip into a large serving bowl.

A wonderfully, luxurious dish that is perfect for a picnic accompanied by a cold glass of Sancerre. Fresh white crabmeat is sometimes difficult to obtain – frozen or pasturized is not too bad though it will need a good squeeze once defrosted. We sometimes omit the saffron and top the tart with grated Gruyère cheese for a change. I think this is best served warm.

Crab, Tomato and Saffron Tart

SERVES 8

1 quantity Savoury Pastry (see page 155), at room temperature

Flour for dusting

1tbsp lemon juice

1tsp saffron threads

1tbsp butter

4 spring onions, trimmed and finely chopped

Salt and pepper

6 egg yolks

425ml double cream

400g cooked white crabmeat

1tbsp parsley

2tbsp finely chopped chives

3tbsp Slow-cooked Tomato Sauce (see page 154) or cooked tomatoes

Thinly roll out the pastry on a lightly floured board using a floured rolling pin, and use to line a 28-cm tart ring, leaving a 1-cm overhang. Leave to rest for 30 minutes in the fridge. Meanwhile, preheat the oven to 190°C/375°F/Gas Mark 5. Blind bake the tart case (see page 12) for 10 minutes. Remove the baking beans and paper and return the tart case to the oven for a further 10–15 minutes, or until lightly golden brown. Put the tart case aside.

While the pastry is baking, warm the lemon juice and add the saffron, then leave to infuse for at least 30 minutes. (Soaking saffron in warm liquid intensifies the colour and flavour.)

In a small saucepan, melt the butter, add the spring onions, season with salt and pepper and fry gently for 5 minutes.

Beat the egg yolks and cream together in a large bowl. Fold in the saffron-flavoured lemon juice, the spring onions, crab and herbs. Taste and season with salt and pepper – exercise caution as the crab can be quite salty. Spread the tomato sauce in the bottom of the tart case (alternatively, put slices of tomato on top of the tart if you do not have any sauce to hand). Pour in the crab mixture, smooth the surface with the back of a spoon and bake for about 20 minutes, or until the tart is set.

Remove the tart from the oven. Trim off the overhanging pastry with a sharp, serrated knife and ease the tart on to a serving plate. Leave the tart to rest for 10 minutes before serving.

Try this for an elegant, easy starter or light lunch. If you have never made a terrine before, this is a good one to start with. It is fairly foolproof, but you need to be bold with the seasoning. This must be made at least one day in advance before eating. Serve with toast, chutney and salad. You will need a 26 x 8 x 7-cm terrine mould – I think the "Le Creuset" brand is best.

Chicken and Parma Ham Terrine

SERVES 10

Oil for oiling

12 slices of Parma ham

8 boneless and skinless chicken breasts

2 egg yolks

145ml single cream

Salt and pepper

2tbsp finely chopped shallot

1½tbsp finely chopped tarragon

Preheat the oven to 150°C/375°F/Gas Mark 5. Lightly oil the inside of the terrine mould then line with clingfilm. Pull it lengthways, pushing down to the corners and edges to remove any trapped air. There should be an overhang of at least 5cm all round. Lay the ham on top of the clingfilm with their edges slightly overlapping; do not put any ham at the ends. There should be an overhang of at least 4cm on both sides.

Using a sharp, thin-bladed carving knife, slice the breasts lengthways as if you were slicing smoked salmon. You should aim for 3 slices per breast, about 3mm in thickness. Place the egg yolks and cream in a bowl and beat together. Season generously, then add the shallots, tarragon and chicken and combine thoroughly – use your hands to do this.

Start putting in layers of the chicken mix, one layer at a time. Try not to leave any gaps and be careful to ensure an even distribution of the cream. When all the chicken is in, fold over the overhanging Parma ham to make a neat parcel. Do the same with the clingfilm, starting with the sides first then folding over the ends. Cover with foil and place the lid on top. Place the terrine in a roasting tray, slightly larger than the terrine. Pour boiling water around the terrine so that it comes up to just below the top. Carefully place on the middle shelf of the oven and bake for 1 hour. Remove the tray from the oven and insert a skewer into the centre of the terrine and count to 10. Put the skewer on the bottom of your lower lip and if hot, it is cooked. If warm, or you are in doubt, cook for longer.

Remove from the oven and take off the lid. Cut a piece of cardboard to a shape slightly smaller than the top of the terrine and place on top. Weigh it down with 2 small cans and leave for 24 hours. Remove the terrine from its mould and turn out on to a serving dish or chopping board.

Most people love a prawn sandwich. This recipe uses the curried mayonnaise from the 1970s classic lunch party staple, coronation chicken. The idea comes courtesy of Simon Hopkinson's much-missed column in the **Independent** and it is quite delicious. This recipe may make more mayonnaise than you need – the extra will keep well for a week if refrigerated.

Open Sandwich of Prawns, Curried Mayonnaise and Baby Gem

SERVES 4

400g Norwegian prawns, peeled (thawed if frozen)

1 baby Gem lettuce, finely shredded

1tbsp chopped coriander

Butter

Wholemeal bread, thickly sliced

For the curried mayonnaise

150ml vegetable oil

2tbsp finely chopped onion

1 garlic clove, finely chopped

1tbsp mild curry powder

2 egg yolks

1tbsp mango chutney

½tsp Dijon mustard

Juice of 1 lime

Salt and pepper

To make the mayonnaise, put the oil, onion and garlic into a small saucepan and simmer over a gentle heat for 30 minutes, stirring from time to time. Add the curry powder and cook for a further 5 minutes. Tip the contents of the pan into a sturdy sieve and push the oil through with the back of a ladle. Discard the onion mixture and leave the oil to cool.

Put the egg yolks, mango chutney, mustard and lime juice into the bowl of a food processor, season with salt and pepper and pulse until smooth. With the motor running, add the oil – drop by drop to start with – and then in a steady stream until you have a thickish mayonnaise. Cover and chill if not using at once.

Give the prawns a squeeze to remove any excess moisture. Combine the lettuce, coriander, prawns and mayonnaise in a bowl and season with salt and pepper. Pile the prawn mixture high on to buttered slices of wholemeal bread.

A felicitous combination if ever there was one. It is important to have a high ratio of clams to pasta. The sweetest, juiciest clams are "palourdes" – extremely expensive but by far the best. See page 15 for the best way to clean clams. The recipe works equally well without the bacon.

Spaghetti with Clams, Smoked Bacon and Garlic

SERVES 4

250g spaghetti

Salt and pepper

200g smoked bacon, finely chopped

200g smoked bacon, finely chopped

Olive oil

1.5kg clams

100ml dry white wine

80g butter

3 garlic cloves, finely chopped

1tbsp chopped parsley

To cook the spaghetti, put a large pan of salted water on to boil.

In a large saucepan, fry the bacon in a little olive oil over a moderate heat until tender. Add the clams and the white wine, turn the heat up to full and cover with a tight-fitting lid. Leave the clams to steam for 2 or 3 minutes, or until the clams are open. Drain the contents of the pan into a colander suspended over a bowl. Have a quick check to make sure there are no unopened clams – discard these if you find them.

Meanwhile, add the spaghetti to the boiling water and cook until al dente.

Melt the butter in the pan in which you cooked the clams. Add the garlic and fry for 2 minutes without colouring. Add the bacon and clams, season with pepper and tip in the drained pasta. Add about half of the reserved clam juices, bearing in mind that they will be salty. You may need to lubricate the dish with additional butter or olive oil.

Turn the spaghetti and clams into a large serving bowl and strew with chopped parsley. This is a dish to get stuck into, so serve finger bowls.

Skate cheeks (sometimes known as skate knobs) are delicious – delicate and succulent. They can be hard to get hold of, so use any firm-fleshed, white fish as a substitute. Use bitter or lager for the batter, or coat the cheeks in breadcrumbs instead of the batter. This mayonnaise is a neat variation on tartare sauce. The recipe requires a deep-fat fryer.

Beer-battered Skate Cheeks with Pickled Onion and Parsley Mayonnaise

SERVES 4

Vegetable oil for deep-frying

500g skate cheeks

Seasoned plain flour

For the beer batter

14g (2 sachets) dried yeast

165ml bitter or lager

110g plain flour

For the parsley mayonnaise

80ml Mayonnaise (see page 153)

2tbsp chopped flat-leaf parsley

2tbsp neatly chopped pickled onion

1tsp capers, finely chopped

First make the batter. Dissolve the yeast into the beer then slowly whisk in the flour. Put the batter to one side to rest for 30 minutes.

Meanwhile, make the mayonnaise by mixing all the ingredients together in a bowl.

Preheat your deep-fat fryer to its maximum setting with enough oil for deep-frying.

Prepare the skate. Using a small, sharp knife, remove the skin and any cartilage (freeze these trimmings for your next fish stock). Cut the fish into bite-sized pieces, then dredge lightly in seasoned flour. Give the batter a quick stir before dropping the fish into it. Using a pair of tongs, place the fish – a few pieces at a time – directly into the oil and deep-fry until golden brown, about 3–4 minutes. Drain on kitchen paper and keep warm while you fry the remaining cheeks. Serve with a ramekin of the mayonnaise and a wedge of lemon.

GRILLS

Perfect barbecue food, this dish is clean-tasting and full of contrasting textures and flavours. The Vietnamese wrap the chicken in lettuce leaves and season with crushed peanuts, fresh herbs, sliced spring onion and cucumber and then dip in the hot-and-sour sauce. Cook on a barbecue or in a frying pan.

Vietnamese Chicken Patties with Lime Dipping Sauce

SERVES 4

450g minced chicken

1tbsp very finely chopped lemon grass bulb

½ green chilli, deseeded and finely chopped

2tbsp Thai fish sauce

4tbsp blanched, roasted peanuts, ground to a powder

3tbsp very finely chopped shallot

1tsp mild curry powder

1tsp caster sugar

3tbsp thick coconut milk or cream

Vegetable oil for brushing

A selection of cucumber slices, spring onions, lettuce leaves, crushed toasted peanuts, beansprouts, mint and coriander leaves

For the lime dipping sauce

5tbsp Thai fish sauce

3tbsp rice wine vinegar or white wine vinegar

2tbsp lime juice

2tbsp caster sugar

1 green chilli, deseeded and cut across into thin slices

To make the chicken patties, combine all the ingredients and mix well. Shape into miniature hamburgers, about 1.5 cm thick. (Dipping your hands into a bowl of water first will help.) Brush each one with oil, put on a tray and refrigerate until needed.

To make the dipping sauce, combine all the ingredients in a non-reactive bowl and leave to infuse for an hour.

Remove the chicken patties from the fridge about an hour before you plan to start cooking. Preheat the barbecue.

When the barbecue is hot, brush the bars with oil and grill the chicken patties on both sides until lightly golden. Depending on the thickness, it should take 2–3 minutes each side. If in doubt, cut one in half to check if it is done. Transfer the patties to a serving plate with the vegetables and dipping sauce and allow your guests to help themselves.

This is a robust salad with plenty of flavour from the tomatoes and olives. Use baby artichokes that have been chargrilled and marinated in olive oil (normally available from good delis). The marinade of lemon, garlic and thyme gives the monkfish a wonderful flavour. Ideally, it needs to be marinated for at least 12 hours.

Warm Salad of Grilled Monkfish and Baby Artichokes

SERVES 4

grated rind of 1 lemon

1tbsp chopped thyme

2 garlic cloves, grated

½tsp crushed black pepper

2tbsp olive oil

4 monkfish fillets (about 150g each)

Vegetable oil for cooking

For the artichoke salad

2tbsp lemon juice

½ red onion, finely sliced

½ garlic clove, finely chopped

½tsp caster sugar

3tbsp stoned black olives, sliced

Salt and pepper

100g baby artichokes, quartered

150g Roast Tomatoes (see page 152), peeled and chopped

100ml olive oil

4tbsp extra virgin olive oil

100g extra-fine green beans, topped and tailed, cooked, refreshed and cooled

1 bunch of flat-leaf parsley, picked, rinsed and spun

Make the marinade by combining the lemon rind, thyme, garlic, pepper and olive oil.

Most monkfish has already been skinned but there is usually a thin outer membrane, which also needs to be removed. Either get the fishmonger to do it or proceed yourself by holding each fillet by its tail, skin-side down, and running a sharp knife under the membrane. Push the knife away from you as you hold on to the skin. Now slice the monkfish into 4-cm pieces and add to the marinade. Mix thoroughly, cover and refrigerate for at least 12 hours.

Make the salad an hour before you eat to give the flavours plenty of time to blend. In a non-reactive bowl, combine the lemon juice with the onion, garlic, sugar and olives and season generously with salt and pepper. Leave for 10 minutes. Now add the artichokes, tomatoes and both olive oils and give everything a good stir. Just before you start cooking the monkfish, add the green beans and parsley, season with salt, toss and put on to a serving platter.

To cook the monkfish, place a ridged grill pan or heavy-bottomed frying pan over a high heat and leave for 5 minutes to get red hot. Remove the monkfish from the fridge and pat the pieces dry. Brush them with a little oil, season with salt and, using a pair of tongs, place on the pan. Do not touch for 2–3 minutes, by which time they will need turning over. Cook for a further 2 minutes until both sides are golden brown and charred in places. Serve immediately with the salad.

Squid has become popular and consequently it is not as cheap as it used to be. To save the messy business of cleaning the squid, look for squid tubes that have already been prepared. Frozen squid is not suitable for this recipe. The chickpea purée is a toned down version of houmous – its texture contrasts nicely with the slight chewiness of the squid.

Chargrilled Squid, Chickpea Purée, Roasted Pepper and Lemon Salsa

SERVES 4

400g squid, lightly scored on the inside

Salt and pepper

For the pepper salsa

1 large red pepper

1 lemon

½ red chilli, deseeded and finely chopped

1tbsp chopped parsley

1tbsp chopped coriander

3tbsp olive oil, plus extra for brushing

For the chickpea purée

1tsp cumin seeds

1tsp coriander seeds

350g drained, cooked chickpeas

1 garlic clove, peeled and grated

1tsp tahini paste or sesame oil

2tbsp olive oil

5tbsp water

Start by grilling the pepper for the salsa. Put a ridged grill pan or heavy-bottomed frying pan on to a high heat and leave for 5 minutes to get red hot. Cut off the stalk and rub a little oil into the pepper. Grill until all sides are blistered and blackened. Pop into a sealed plastic bag and leave to cool. Remove the skin and seeds as much as possible, chop into 3-mm dice and place in a mixing bowl. Using a sharp knife, cut off the lemon rind and pith. Segment the flesh, remove any pips, dice into 3-mm pieces and add to the peppers. Combine the other ingredients and season with salt and pepper. Leave to infuse for half an hour.

Meanwhile, make the purée. "Dry roast" the spices until they emit a pleasant aroma, about 2 minutes on a moderate heat. Remove and grind finely. Place the chickpeas, the spices, garlic, tahini, olive oil and water into a blender and process until smooth.

Preheat a ridged grill pan or heavy-bottomed frying pan until it is hot. Pat the squid dry, lightly oil both sides and season with salt and pepper. Using a pair of tongs, put the squid on to the pan and cook for 2 minutes before turning. Cook the second side for a minute. Serve immediately with the chickpea purée, a few rocket leaves and the salsa spooned on top.

Scallops are best with something creamy with a bit of texture and these lentils are perfect. Do be careful when you buy scallops. Fishmongers can get up to all sorts of tricks, including soaking scallops in water to bulk out their weight. Really fresh scallops will be firm and opalescent. Be wary of anything sitting in water and avoid scallops that have been previously frozen.

Griddled Scallops with Spiced Red Lentils

SERVES 4

125g red lentils

1 onion, finely chopped

3tbsp vegetable oil, plus extra
   for brushing

4 garlic cloves, finely chopped

2.5-cm piece of ginger, chopped

1 carrot, grated

250g canned chopped tomatoes

1 small bunch of coriander, leaves
   removed and chopped, stalks and
   roots tied into a bundle

200ml water

100ml coconut milk

Juice of ½ lemon

500g medium or large shucked
   scallops

Salt

For the spice mixture

2tsp coriander seeds

2tsp cumin seeds

3 cloves

2.5-cm piece of cinnamon stick

1tbsp yellow mustard seeds

½tbsp cardamom seeds

1 small dried red chilli

1 bay leaf

1tsp black peppercorns

Start by soaking the lentils. Cover them with double their volume of water and put to one side for 30 minutes.

Meanwhile, make the spice mix. Dry roast the spices in a small frying pan over a moderate heat for 2 minutes until you get a pleasant "toasted" aroma and the seeds start to pop. Transfer to a grinder or a pestle and mortar and grind until fine. Put to one side.

In a heavy-bottomed saucepan, fry the onion in the oil for 10 minutes over a moderate heat until starting to colour. Reduce the heat to low, add the garlic, ginger and carrot and fry for a further 10 minutes, stirring occasionally. Add the drained lentils, tomatoes, coriander bundle and water. Bring to the boil, then reduce the heat and simmer over a low heat for about 1½ hours. It is important to stir the pan every 5 minutes or so otherwise the lentils are likely to catch. If the lentils are looking on the dry side, add more water. When the lentils have collapsed and don't have any bite to them, add the coconut milk and lemon juice. Cook for 2 minutes then remove the pan from the heat. Season heavily with salt, stir well and leave for 2 minutes. Taste again and adjust the seasoning, if necessary. Fold in 2 tablespoons of the chopped coriander leaves.

Place a heavy-bottomed frying pan or ridged grill pan over a high heat and leave for 5 minutes to get red hot. You may need to heat more than one pan to prevent the scallops from getting overcrowded. Make sure the scallops are dry then brush them with a little oil. Using a pair of tongs, place the scallops into the pan and cook each side until crusty and golden brown, about 1½ minutes on each side. Adjust the heat, if necessary, to avoid burning. Season both sides with salt. Serve with the lentils, lightly cooked spinach and a wedge of lemon.

This is a delicious combination full of contrasting flavours and textures. The sweetness of the beetroot is countered by the salty bacon, the sharp sorrel and the perkiness of the horseradish. Ask your fishmonger to slice the sea trout across the grain into thin 1-cm escalopes.

Sea Trout with Beetroot, Bacon, Sorrel and Horseradish

SERVES 4

300g beetroot

Salt and pepper

1 small bunch of fresh dill

2tbsp finely chopped shallot

2tbsp lemon juice

½tsp caster sugar

½tsp Dijon mustard

2tbsp grated horseradish

1tbsp crème fraîche or soured cream

6tbsp olive oil

Vegetable oil for cooking

150g smoked bacon, diced

100g extra-fine green beans or shelled peas (frozen are fine), cooked and cooled

1 bunch of watercress, rinsed and spun

4 sea trout escalopes (about 150g each)

3tbsp shredded sorrel leaves

Put the beetroot into a pan, cover with cold water and season heavily with salt. Add the stalks from the dill and bring to the boil. Simmer for about 2 hours, or until the blade of small, sharp knife goes easily into the beetroot. Drain and leave to cool, then peel and slice into 1-cm wedges. Put to one side. (The beetroot can be prepared up to 2 days in advance.)

To make the dressing, combine the shallot, lemon juice, sugar, mustard and horseradish in a non-reactive bowl. Add a teaspoon of chopped dill to the bowl, season with salt and pepper and leave to blend for 5 minutes. Now whisk in the crème fraîche and olive oil until you have a thin creamy dressing.

Pour a little vegetable oil into a frying pan and cook the bacon over a moderately high heat until it is tender and golden on all sides. Using a slotted spoon, transfer the bacon to a piece of kitchen paper and keep warm while you assemble the salad.

When you are ready to cook the sea trout, add the beetroot and green beans to the bowl with the dressing. Tip the salad on to a bed of watercress.

Put a heavy-bottomed frying pan or ridged grill pan over a high heat and leave for 5 minutes until it is hot. Oil the fish lightly on both sides and season with salt and pepper. Cook for 1 minute on each side: you are aiming for the centre of the fish to be slightly underdone. Scatter the bacon and sorrel over the salad and serve immediately.

Mackerel, being oily, is the perfect fish to grill. The smoked paprika and salt rub works well for most types of oily fish and this recipe is one of our top sellers. There are two varieties of pimentón (Spanish smoked paprika) – mild and hot – use the mild for this dish. I wouldn't recommend doing this indoors unless you have an extremely efficient extraction system.

Grilled Mackerel with Smoked Paprika and Sea Salt, with a White Bean, Roasted Pepper and Cucumber Salad

SERVES 4

1½tbsp red wine vinegar

½tsp caster sugar

1 small red onion, finely sliced

1 garlic clove, finely chopped

1tsp bottled capers, rinsed and finely chopped

Salt and pepper

2 roasted red peppers (see page 14), cored

180g canned white beans, drained and rinsed

2tbsp chopped basil

2tbsp chopped flat-leaf parsley

3tbsp extra virgin olive oil

3tbsp olive oil

4 large mackerel, gutted and trimmed

Vegetable oil for brushing

2tsp smoked paprika

2tsp sea salt

Start by making the salad, which needs to be made at least an hour in advance. In a non-reactive bowl, mix the red wine vinegar, sugar, onion, garlic and capers. Season liberally with salt and pepper and leave for 20 minutes to get the flavours to exchange. Add the peppers, beans, herbs and olive oils and mix thoroughly, then put to one side.

Meanwhile, preheat your grill, or a ridged grill pan, or heat your barbecue coals until glowing.

Take the mackerel, wipe dry and slash the fish, making 3 or 4 incisions on both sides. Rub a little vegetable oil on to each fish and then add the paprika, rubbing lightly on to the skin and into the slashes. When you are ready to cook, grill the mackerel for about 5 minutes on each side. It doesn't matter – in fact it is desirable – if the fish ends up charred in places. Crunch up the sea salt between your thumb and fingers and sprinkle over the fish. Using a pair of tongs, place the fish on to a serving plate and serve with wedges of lemon.

This is a fabulous recipe, which my children adore. I'm afraid it takes days to prepare but persevere and you will be well-rewarded. The plum sauce is really worth making and works brilliantly with the pork. Serve with a dressed salad of baby Gem lettuce, carrot, cucumber and spring onion.

Twice-cooked Belly of Pork with Home-made Plum Sauce

SERVES 4–6

1 belly of pork (about 2.5kg)

Vegetable oil for cooking

For the marinade

2.5-cm piece of ginger, finely grated

4 garlic cloves, finely grated

6tbsp light soy sauce

3tbsp dry sherry

2tbsp rice wine vinegar or white
  wine vinegar

2tbsp clear honey

5tbsp orange juice

For the plum sauce

1tbsp vegetable oil

½ red onion, very finely chopped

1.5-cm piece of ginger, very
  finely chopped

1 garlic clove, grated

1 red chilli, deseeded and
  finely chopped

2tsp rinsed and finely chopped
  coriander root

½ star anise

100g caster sugar

400g plums, halved and stoned

½tbsp light soy sauce

1tsp Thai fish sauce

2 tbsp chopped coriander

Slow roast the belly of pork following the instructions on page 132 and leave the belly to cool. Put it on to a chopping board and examine the crackling. If good, leave it on – otherwise remove with a sharp knife and discard. Now, pull out the ribs and slice the pork into 2-cm thick slices.

Put the marinade ingredients into a non-reactive bowl and whisk until combined. Tip the pork slices into the bowl and mix carefully to ensure each slice is coated. Put the contents of the bowl into a large, sealed plastic bag and refrigerate for up to 48 hours.

Meanwhile, to make the sauce, heat the oil in a roomy saucepan over a high heat. Add the onion, ginger, garlic, chilli, coriander root and star anise and cook briskly for 3 minutes, stirring frequently. Now pour in the sugar and continue to cook over a high heat until the sugar dissolves. Just as the sugar is about to change colour, about 5 minutes, throw in the plums and bring to a simmer. Simmer for about 10 minutes, or until the plums are just beginning to collapse: you are aiming for a chunky sauce. (The plums should be undercooked – they will continue to soften in the residual heat.) Stir in the soy sauce, fish sauce and chopped coriander. Put aside and leave to cool.

It is best to cook the pork on a barbecue but it also works under a grill. Remove the pork from the fridge at least an hour before you wish to eat. Scrape off the marinade and lightly oil the pork on each side. Grill until both sides are well-coloured, about 6 minutes altogether.

This fennel salad is clean, superbly refreshing and goes well with any oily fish, such as mackerel, salmon or trout. It is best served chilled. Sardines are not the best thing to grill indoors unless you have a state-of-the-art extraction system. It is important the grill is clean before you add the sardines.

Grilled Sardines with Marinated Fennel and Lemon Salad

SERVES 4

Vegetable oil for brushing

8 sardines, scaled and gutted

Salt and pepper

For the fennel and lemon salad

400g fennel

Juice of 1 lemon

2 garlic cloves, sliced

6tbsp extra virgin olive oil

2tbsp chopped flat-leaf parsley

Make the salad an hour before you wish to eat. Using a small sharp knife, trim the base and any blemished outside leaves of the fennel. Cut off the stalks and retain the bright green fronds. (Freeze the trimmings for your next fish stock.) Using a mandolin or a heavy knife, horizontally slice the fennel wafer thin. Put into a bowl and add the lemon juice and garlic, then season generously with sea salt and pepper. Give the ingredients a good toss, leave to marinate for 30 minutes and then chill. Just before serving, add the olive oil, parsley and the chopped fennel fronds. Taste and adjust the seasoning if necessary (it should be quite tart).

Preheat the grill to high and lightly brush the grill rack with oil.

Place the sardines on a plate and rub oil on to both sides, then season with salt and pepper and grill for about 5 minutes until both sides are cooked. Taste and adjust the seasoning of the salad, if necessary and serve alongside the hot sardines.

This is a marvellous combination: sweet, caramelized pork with sharp, crunchy celeriac and apple. Marinate the pork at least a day ahead for best results. Serve with a salad of dressed watercress, finely sliced shallots and some green beans. Start this recipe a day in advance.

Treacle-marinated Pork Chops with Apple and Celeriac Salad

SERVES 4

4 pork chops (each about 2.5cm thick), trimmed and skin removed

Vegetable oil for brushing

Salt and pepper

For the marinade

1 tbsp black treacle

1 small onion, coarsely grated

1tbsp soy sauce
2 juniper berries, crushed

150ml bitter or dry cider

1tbsp soft brown sugar

½tsp black peppercorns, crushed

For the celeriac salad

300g celeriac

6 tbsp Mayonnaise (see page 153)

1½tsp Dijon mustard

2 dessert apples, cored and thinly sliced

1tbsp chopped chives

In a non-reactive mixing bowl, combine the marinade ingredients. Rub the marinade into the pork chops, then transfer to a large, sealed plastic bag and refrigerate for 24 hours.

Meanwhile, to make the salad, peel and shred the celeriac into thin matchsticks (a mandolin is ideal for this), combine in a bowl together with the other salad ingredients and season with salt and pepper. The salad should be quite mustardy. Leave to one side while you cook the chops.

Remove the pork from the fridge at least an hour before you plan to eat. Preheat the grill to its maximum setting. Scrape off the marinade and discard. Brush the chops lightly with oil and season with salt. Place under the grill for about 5 minutes on each side, or until cooked through and tender. Do not put the chops too close to the grill or else they will burn – 12cm below the grill is about right. Leave to rest for 5 minutes in a warm place before serving.

Marinate the lamb for at least a day to allow the onion to tenderize the meat and for the flavours to marry. The kebabs are best cooked on a barbecue but an ordinary grill is fine. The pilaff rice is utterly delicious and good enough to eat on its own. It can be made with water but is much better with chicken stock. Serve with minted yoghurt and a cucumber and tomato salad.

Lamb, Aubergine and Red Onion Kebab with Pilaff Rice

SERVES 4

700g boneless leg of lamb, cut into 3-cm chunks

2 red onions, quartered

300g aubergine, cut into 3-cm chunks

Vegetable oil for brushing

Salt and pepper

For the marinade

1 small onion, finely grated

4tbsp grated garlic

1tbsp finely chopped rosemary

Juice of ½ lemon

3tbsp olive oil

For the pilaff rice

425g basmati rice, soaked in water for 30 minutes

3tbsp vegetable oil

½ small onion, finely chopped

1 garlic clove, finely chopped

½ green chilli, deseeded and finely chopped

½tsp garam masala

600ml chicken stock

Start by marinating the lamb at least 24 hours ahead of time. Combine the marinade ingredients in a non-reactive bowl and stir in the lamb. Tip into a large, sealed plastic bag and refrigerate until needed.

Before you start the kebabs, cook and drain the rice, preheat the oven to 200°C/400°F/Gas Mark 6 and heat the barbecue coals until glowing.

Put the oil in a flameproof casserole and cook the onion over a moderate heat for about 10 minutes until they start to colour. Add the garlic and chilli and cook for a further minute. Now stir in the drained rice and stir-fry the rice in the oil for a further 3 minutes, making sure it is glossy and well coated. Add the garam masala, the chicken stock and a generous amount of salt. Bring to the boil, cover with a circle of greaseproof paper and a tight-fitting lid and place in the top of the oven to bake for about 15 minutes. Remove from the oven and check to see that all the liquid has been absorbed. Fluff up the rice with a fork.

To make the kebabs, scrape the marinade from the lamb. Start and finish the kebabs with a red onion "stopper". Alternate the lamb, aubergine and red onion as you wish. Keep the sides of the kebabs as even as possible, leaving a small gap between each piece.

When the barbecue is hot, lightly oil the bars of the grill, brush the kebabs with oil and season with salt and pepper. Using a pair of tongs, cook the kebabs, turning every 2 minutes to cook each side until the vegetables are lightly charred and the lamb is pink in the middle. Serve with the warm rice.

Known as "skirt steak" in the UK, at The Havelock we sell more bavette than anything else. To my mind, no steak tastes more flavoursome. There is a drawback: it must be cooked rare. Marinate the steak at least one day in advance. The butter is delicious and comes from Joanne Wilkinson, one of the finest chefs I know. You can make the butter up to three days in advance.

Grilled Bavette Steak with Tomato and Tarragon Butter

SERVES 4

For the marinade

4 x 150g bavette steak

4 garlic cloves, crushed

½ onion, finely sliced

½ bunch of thyme

4tbsp olive oil

½tsp crushed black pepper

For the tomato butter

150g softened butter

2 Roast Tomatoes (see page 152), peeled and finely chopped

1tbsp shallot, finely chopped

½tsp garlic, grated

1tbsp tarragon, finely chopped

2tsp light soy sauce

Salt

Put the steaks into a bowl and rub the marinade ingredients all over. Tip into a sealed plastic bag and refrigerate for 24 hours.

Meanwhile, make the butter. Put all the ingredients into a bowl, season with a little salt (watch the saltiness of the soy) and beat with a wooden spoon. Set aside. Note: in place of the roast tomatoes, cook 2 chopped tomatoes in butter until they are well reduced.

To cook the steaks, remove from the fridge at least half an hour before eating. Scrape off the onion, garlic and thyme and discard. Put a heavy-bottomed frying pan or ridged grill pan over a high heat and leave to get hot for at least 5 minutes.

Rub a little more olive oil onto each side and season with salt. Using a pair of tongs, grill the steaks on each side until rare – about 5 minutes in total. Check by giving one of the steaks a squeeze between thumb and forefinger: it should still feel quite soft. Leave to rest in a warm place for 5 minutes. Carve across the grain in thin 3-mm slices. Serve with the melted butter and a salad of watercress, shallots and green beans.

The chicken needs to be prepared one day in advance to allow the marinade to work. Spatchcocking the chicken is not difficult, you just need a decent pair of scissors. Buying a whole bird also works out cheaper than individual joints. The chicken can be cooked on a barbecue but unless you are careful, it is liable to stick and burn.

Spatchcocked Chicken Marinated with Yoghurt

SERVES 4

1 free-range chicken (about 1.5kg)

Juice of 1½ lemons

9tbsp natural yoghurt

4-cm piece of ginger, peeled and finely grated

5 garlic cloves, finely grated

½ small onion, finely grated

1½tsp ground cumin

1 red chilli, deseeded and finely chopped

¼tsp garam masala

3tbsp vegetable oil

Salt

Using a pair of sharp scissors, cut out the backbone from the chicken and lay it breast-side up on a board. Using the heel of your hand, crush the breast plate until the chicken is flat. Use a sharp knife to slash the chicken all over with small incisions, particularly around the thighs and legs, then put to one side.

To make the marinade, combine all the remaining ingredients in a non-reactive bowl and season heavily with salt. Work this mixture into the chicken, pushing the marinade into the slashes, then cover and refrigerate for 24 hours.

Bring the chicken to room temperature an hour before you start cooking, and preheat the grill to its highest setting.

Place the chicken on a baking tray on the top shelf of the oven and grill for 15 minutes, skin-side up. Turn over and cook for a further 15 minutes. If the chicken is cooking too fast, reduce the heat of the grill and place the chicken on a lower shelf. Check that the chicken is cooked by inserting a skewer into the thickest part of the leg – if the juices run clear, it is cooked. Leave the chicken to rest in a warm place for 5 minutes before slicing and serving.

CURRIES

This is a Thai version of a Moslem curry, rich in spices but quite mild and a little sweet. The chillies to use are the long, thin ones (the small bird's-eye variety will blow your head off). The recipe yields more curry paste than you'll need – refrigerate the leftover under a thin film of oil or freeze for future use. Serve this curry with plain, steamed rice and toasted crushed peanuts.

Mussaman Beef Curry with Toasted Peanuts

SERVES 4

800g chuck steak

6tbsp vegetable oil

2 onions, quartered

3tbsp Mussaman Curry Paste

600ml coconut milk

2tsp palm sugar or soft brown sugar

2tsp tamarind paste or lemon juice

4tbsp Thai fish sauce

200g new potatoes

Salt

Blanched peanuts, roasted

Chopped coriander

For the mussaman curry paste

25 large, dried red chillies

1 lemon grass bulb, chopped

4 shallots, sliced

5 garlic cloves, sliced

1tbsp peeled and chopped kra-chai

10 kaffir lime leaves, chopped

1tbsp chopped coriander root

1tbsp ground coriander

1tsp ground cumin

½tsp ground cinnamon

1tsp palm sugar or soft brown sugar

½tsp trassi (dried shrimp paste)

2tbsp vegetable oil

Preheat the oven to 150°C/300°F/Gas Mark 2.

To make the paste, deseed the chillies and put all the ingredients including the chillies and 1 teaspoon salt into the bowl of a blender and process until completely smooth, scraping the sides of the bowl, if necessary. Put to one side. Note: If kra-chai is unavailable then use ginger or galangal and if you cannot buy trassi use ½ teaspoon salt.

Cut the steak into 5-cm chunks. In a large, heavy-bottomed frying pan, heat half of the oil over a high heat. Fry the beef – in 2 or 3 batches, if necessary – and brown evenly on all sides. Put the beef to one side.

Add the remaining oil to a flameproof casserole and cook the onions over a high heat for 5 minutes, stirring. Turn down the heat and stir in the curry paste for 2–3 minutes, or until it bubbles. Add the beef and any accumulated juices to the casserole, then stir in the coconut milk, sugar, tamarind and fish sauce and bring to the boil. Remove the casserole from the heat and cover with foil and a tight-fitting lid. Place the casserole in the middle shelf of the oven and cook for 2 hours, or until the beef is tender.

Meanwhile, cook, peel and chop the new potatoes. Twenty minutes before the end of the allotted cooking time, remove the casserole from the oven and add the cooked potatoes. Quickly bring the liquid back to a simmer and return the casserole to the oven.

Taste and adjust the seasoning if necessary by adding more salt. Turn into a serving dish, chop the peanuts then strew over with the coriander.

This very hot curry is from the former Portuguese colony of Goa, where it is usually made with pork but also with duck, beef and lamb. (The name derives from the Portuguese word for wine, "vinho", and for garlic, "alhos".) The basic technique involves making a vindaloo paste consisting of fried onions, vinegar and spices, which can be made in advance and frozen.

Hot-and-Sour Pork Curry with Raita (Vindaloo)

SERVES 4

2.5-cm piece of ginger, chopped

10 garlic cloves, peeled but whole

900g boneless neck or shoulder of pork, cut into 5-cm pieces

300ml chicken stock

Salt and pepper

For the vindaloo paste

2tsp cumin seeds

3 dried red chillies

1tsp black peppercorns

1tsp cardamom seeds

2-cm piece of cinnamon stick

1½tsp black mustard seeds

1tsp fenugreek seeds

1tbsp coriander seeds

10tbsp vegetable oil

2 onions, finely sliced

5tbsp white wine vinegar

1tsp soft brown sugar

½tsp turmeric

6tbsp water

For the raita

½ cucumber, deseeded and grated

300ml natural yoghurt

1 tbsp chopped mint

Pinch of cayenne pepper

Preheat the oven to 150°C/300°F/Gas Mark 2. To make the vindaloo paste, dry-roast the cumin, chillies, peppercorns, cardamom, cinnamon, mustard seeds, fenugreek and coriander in a small frying pan over a moderate heat for about 2 minutes until you get a pleasant "roasted" aroma. Transfer the spices to a grinder or pestle and mortar and grind finely. Put to one side.

In a large frying pan, heat the half of the oil until hot. Add the onions and fry until they are crispy and brown, which usually takes about 30 minutes over a moderate heat. Place the onions, the vinegar, sugar and turmeric into a blender. Add half of the water and some salt and blend to a smooth paste, scraping down the sides of the blender, if necessary. Tip this mixture into the bowl with the ground spices and mix well. This is the vindaloo paste. Using the same blender (you don't need to wash it), process the ginger, garlic and remaining water until a smooth paste. In a flameproof casserole, heat the remaining oil over a high heat. Fry the pork in 2 or 3 batches until lightly brown all over, then transfer to a plate. Turn the heat down to moderate. Put the ginger-garlic mix in the casserole and stir for a few seconds. Return the pork and any juices to the casserole, together with the vindaloo paste and the stock. Season with salt and pepper and bring to the boil, stirring frequently. Cover with a lid, place on the middle shelf of your oven and cook for 90 minutes, or until the pork is tender. Meanwhile, to make the raita, season the cucumber with salt and drain in a colander for 30 minutes. Give the cucumber a good squeeze and combine with the other ingredients. Season with pepper and more salt if necessary. Cover and chill until required.

Remove from the oven, taste and adjust the seasoning if necessary. Serve with steamed basmati rice and chilled raita.

The recipe for the curry paste will yield more than you need for four people but it keeps for ages – either freeze it or refrigerate under a thin film of oil. For advice about buying scallops, see page 47. Serve with steamed rice, which in Thailand is never cooked with salt. To allow for this, Thai curries should always be highly seasoned.

Thai Yellow Fish Curry with Tiger Prawns and Scallops

SERVES 4

1 large potato

2tbsp vegetable oil

1 onion, finely sliced

500ml coconut milk

4tbsp Thai fish sauce

2tsp palm sugar or soft brown sugar

Juice of 1 lime

100g cherry tomatoes

300g tiger prawns, shelled with head-on

200g scallops, cut into 2.5-cm pieces

2 yellow chillies

Coriander, roughly chopped

For the curry paste

10 yellow chillies

1 lemon grass bulb, chopped

2 shallots, roughly chopped

2tbsp chopped garlic

1tsp ginger

1tsp ground coriander

1tsp ground caraway

1tsp ground cinnamon

1tsp mild curry powder

1tsp ground yellow mustard seeds

1tbsp palm sugar or brown sugar

2tbsp vegetable oil

½tsp trassi or 1tsp salt

To make the curry paste, deseed and roughly chop the chillies then put all the ingredients into the bowl of a blender and process until completely smooth, scraping the sides of the bowl if necessary. Set aside.

To make the curry, peel and cut the potato into 2.5-cm chunks. Heat the oil in a saucepan over a moderate heat. Add the onion and cook for 10 minutes until soft. Add 1½ tablespoons the curry paste and cook for a further 2–3 minutes over a low heat until it starts to bubble. Add the coconut milk, potatoes, fish sauce, sugar and lime juice, stir and bring to the boil.

Turn down the heat to low and simmer until the potatoes are almost cooked (check after 15 minutes). Add the cherry tomatoes, prawns and scallops and bring back to a simmer. Continue to cook for about 5 minutes until the fish is cooked through.

Remove the pan from the heat. Taste and adjust the seasoning by adding more fish sauce, if necessary. Deseed and thinly slice the yellow chillies. Turn the curry into a serving bowl and scatter the chillies and coriander over the top.

TIP: If you cannot find yellow chilli peppers (they are more orange than yellow), use red instead.

You can substitute monkfish for the scallops or pork or chicken for the fish, but you will need to cook the meat from the outset.

If you only make one curry in your life, this is it. It is incredibly good: light and fragrant. The recipe has been adapted from Madhur Jaffrey's **Indian Cookery**, one of my all-time favourite cookbooks. I cannot commend this dish more highly – it is quite superb. I like to serve this with steamed basmati rice and freshly chopped coriander.

Goan Chicken Curry with Roasted Coconut and Fresh Onion Chutney (Shakoothi)

SERVES 4

425g fresh coconut flesh, grated

1½tbsp coriander seeds

1½tsp cumin seeds

1tsp black mustard seeds

½ cinnamon stick

4 cloves

¼tsp black peppercorns

Pinch of grated nutmeg

1 dried red chilli

6 garlic cloves, peeled but left whole

2.5-cm piece of ginger, chopped

1 green chilli, deseeded

125ml water

4tbsp vegetable oil

1 small onion, finely chopped

800g boneless, skinless chicken thighs, each cut into 3 pieces

Salt

215ml chicken stock

For the chutney

110g onion, very finely sliced

4tsp lemon juice

¼tsp paprika

Pinch of cayenne pepper

Preheat the oven to 200°C/400°F/Gas Mark 6. Place the coconut on to a baking sheet and roast in the oven for 10–15 minutes, or until it is golden brown and charred in places. Remove it and put to one side.

Meanwhile, dry-roast the first 8 spices into a small frying pan over a moderate heat for about 2 minutes until you get a pleasant "roasted" aroma (the seeds will be popping slightly). Transfer the spices to a grinder or pestle and mortar and grind them until fine. Put to one side.

Put the garlic, ginger, green chilli and water into a blender and blend until you have a smooth paste.

Heat the oil in a large flameproof casserole over a medium-high heat and fry the onion for 10 minutes until it starts to brown. Now pour in the garlic-ginger paste and stir. Reduce the heat to moderate, add the chicken, the ground spices and the coconut and season generously with salt. Continue to cook, stirring for 4 minutes before adding the chicken stock. Bring to the boil, then cover with foil and a tight-fitting lid. Place the casserole on the middle shelf of the oven and cook for a further 40 minutes, or until the chicken is tender.

Meanwhile, to make the chutney, put all the ingredients including ¾ tablepoon salt into a bowl and mix together. Set aside for 30 minutes to let the flavours blend.

Remove the casserole from the oven, check the seasoning, adding more salt if necessary and serve.

Almost every country has some type of meatball –
these are Indian and quite delicious. Serve with
steamed basmati rice and the tomato relish.

Lamb Koftas with Tomato, Onion and Coriander Relish

SERVES 4

800g minced shoulder of lamb

4tbsp chopped sultanas

4tsp ground cumin

4tsp ground coriander

½tsp garam masala

1¼tsp cayenne pepper

8tbsp finely chopped coriander

5tbsp natural yoghurt

Salt and pepper

For the kofta sauce

10 garlic cloves, peeled but whole

5-cm piece of ginger, chopped

125ml water

125ml vegetable oil

10 cardamom pods

10 cloves

5-cm piece of cinnamon stick

1 large onion, finely chopped

225g canned tomatoes, chopped

125ml natural yoghurt

600ml chicken or lamb stock

For the tomato relish

225g tomatoes, skinned, deseeded
    and cut into 5-mm dice

1 red onion, finely chopped

2tbsp lemon juice

Preheat the oven to 180°C/350°F/Gas Mark 4. To make the koftas, combine the lamb, sultanas, 2 teaspoons each of cumin and coriander, the garam masal, ¼ teaspoon cayenne, half of the coriander and the yoghurt in a bowl and season with salt and pepper. Form into balls the size of a walnut (dipping your hands in a bowl of water whenever you need to will help). Set aside.

To make the sauce, put the garlic, ginger and water into a blender and process until you have a smooth paste. Heat the oil in a flameproof casserole dish over a high heat. When hot, add the cardamom pods, cloves and cinnamon stick, broken into 4 pieces, and stir for a few seconds. Add the onion and continue cooking and stirring for about 10 minutes until they are a rich golden brown. Turn the heat down to medium and stir in the ginger-garlic paste, coriander, cumin and ¼ teaspoon cayenne. Continue to stir for around 30 seconds.

Add the canned tomatoes and cook for a further 5 minutes. Now stir in the yoghurt, a tablespoon at a time to prevent it splitting. When all of the yoghurt has been incorporated, add the stock, season generously with salt, bring to the boil and stir well. Add the meatballs to the casserole in a single layer. Gently bring the sauce back to the boil, cover with a lid and put on to the middle shelf of the oven. Cook for about 1 hour. Meanwhile, to make the relish, place all the ingredients including the remaining ½ teaspoon cayenne in a bowl, season with salt and rest for half an hour.

Remove from the oven. If the sauce is looking a little thin, use a slotted spoon to transfer the meatballs to a plate. Over a high heat reduce the sauce to the desired consistency. Adjust the seasoning if necessary and serve with meatballs and the relish.

Fabulously fragrant, this tagine makes a great Sunday lunch. Mid-neck is easily the best cut for this recipe. The figs can be replaced with dried apricots, prunes or even quince. If you can only find ready-to-eat dried figs, add them half an hour before the end of cooking. Serve with steamed couscous and yoghurt (the yoghurt is not strictly authentic, but delicious nonetheless).

Lamb, Fig and Mint Tagine

SERVES 4

½ tsp saffron threads

1 bunch of coriander

2 tbsp cumin seeds

1 tbsp coriander seeds

8-cm piece of cinnamon stick, broken into 4 pieces

3 tbsp olive oil

1 kg mid-neck or shoulder of lamb, cut into 5-cm chunks

2 onions, finely chopped

3 garlic cloves, finely sliced

2 tbsp tomato purée

500ml chicken or lamb stock

2 carrots, sliced into 4-cm pieces

2 bay leaves

100g canned chickpeas, drained weight, rinsed (optional)

150g dried figs

1½ tbsp dried mint, or 3 tbsp chopped mint

Salt and pepper

Soak the saffron in 2 tablespoons warm water and leave to infuse for at least 30 minutes, although 2 hours is ideal. Pick the coriander leaves off the stalks, chop and reserve for later. Keep the roots and stalks, rinse and carefully tie into a bundle. Put the cumin seeds, coriander seeds and cinnamon into a grinder or pestle and mortar and grind finely. Set aside.

Preheat the oven to 150°C/300°F/Gas Mark 2.

Heat the olive oil in a large, heavy-bottomed frying pan over a high heat. Fry the lamb – in 2 or 3 batches, if necessary – until well browned on all sides. Using a slotted spoon, transfer the lamb to a plate and put to one side. Turn the heat down to low and throw in the onions and garlic. Season generously with salt and pepper and cook for 10 minutes, scraping up any residues from the pan as the onions start to soften.

Add the tomato purée and cook for 2 minutes. Put the onion mixture into a flameproof casserole together with the saffron and coriander stalks. Cover with the stock and add all the remaining ingredients, including the lamb. Bring to the boil, then season with more salt and pepper and cover with a tight-fitting lid. Place the casserole on the middle shelf of the oven and cook for 2 hours.

Remove the casserole from the oven and give everything a good stir. Taste and adjust the seasoning if necessary. Serve garnished with the reserved chopped coriander.

This light, fresh-tasting curry is best served with plain basmati rice, Indian breads and Raita (see page 63). It also works well as an accompaniment for lightly cooked fish and chicken. Ideally use the orange-fleshed sweet potatoes or substitute butternut squash.

Aubergine, Sweet Potato and Cauliflower Curry

SERVES 4

2tsp cumin seeds

1tsp coriander seeds

1 small dried red chilli

1 x 2½-cm cinnamon stick

4tsp black mustard seeds

4 whole garlic cloves

2.5-cm piece of ginger, chopped

3tbsp water

6tbsp vegetable oil

250g aubergine, cut into 3-cm cubes

1 onion, finely chopped

300g sweet potato, peeled and cut into 3-cm cubes

250g cauliflower florets

1 small bunch of coriander, leaves picked and stalks tied into a bundle

1 bay leaf

200ml vegetable stock or water

Salt and pepper

5 tomatoes, skinned, deseeded and quartered

4tbsp coconut milk (optional)

250ml water

Dry-roast the cumin, coriander, chilli, cinnamon stick and mustard seeds in a small frying pan over a moderate heat for about 2 minutes. When the mustard seeds start to pop, remove the pan from the heat. Transfer the spices to a grinder or pestle and mortar and grind them until fine. Put to one side.

Put the garlic, ginger and water into the bowl of a blender or food processor and blend to a smooth paste.

In a large frying pan, heat some of the oil over a high heat. When hot, add the aubergine – in batches if necessary – and fry until golden brown, adding more oil when required (about 2–3 minutes in total). Put the aubergine to one side.

In a heavy-bottomed saucepan, heat more oil, add the onion and soften for 10 minutes over a moderate heat until starting to brown at the edges. Stir in the garlic-ginger paste and fry for a minute. Add the ground spices, sweet potato, cauliflower, coriander stalks, bay leaf and vegetable stock or water. Season generously with salt and pepper. Bring to the boil, then reduce the heat and simmer over a very low heat, partially covered with the lid for 10 minutes. Stir occasionally.

The vegetables should be cooked after 25–30 minutes (test by inserting a small knife into a piece – if it goes in easily, it is cooked). Add the tomatoes and coconut milk. Cook for a further 2 minutes. Remove the pan from the heat, taste and adjust the seasoning, if necessary, by adding more salt.

SUMMER DESSERTS

Sweet and very moreish. I'm afraid, however, you need an ice cream machine to make it.

Honeycomb Crisp Ice Cream with Warm Chocolate Sauce

SERVES 4

For the honeycomb crisp

Vegetable oil for oiling

120g caster sugar

1tbsp golden syrup

30g butter

1tsp bicarbonate of soda

For the chocolate sauce

100ml milk

2tbsp double cream

20g sugar

Small pinch of salt

140g plain dark chocolate

20g butter

Lightly oil a small baking tray.

To make the honeycomb crisp, bring the sugar, golden syrup and butter to the boil in a small saucepan over a high heat, stirring to dissolve the sugar. Reduce the heat and simmer for 5 minutes until it becomes a pale golden brown. Remove the pan from the heat and stir in the bicarbonate of soda – be careful as you do this as the mixture will suddenly froth up (avoid overstirring). Tip the mixture into the baking tray and leave to cool. Once the crisp is completely cool, give the tray a sharp tap and lightly crush the honeycomb into small chunks. Store in a dry, airtight container until ready for use.

Make the ice cream according to the recipe on page 150. Pour the mix into your ice cream machine and churn until thickened. Add the honeycomb crisp at the end then transfer to a freezerproof container and freeze until required.

Meanwhile, to make the chocolate sauce, bring the first 4 ingredients to the boil in a small saucepan. Reduce the heat, add the chocolate and stir over a low heat for 60 seconds. Whisk in the butter, remove the pan from the heat and serve.

TIP: The chocolate sauce will keep in the fridge for up to a week. Once refrigerated, it will solidify – the best way to reheat it is in a covered bowl in the microwave.

Strawberries and oranges are an unusual and delicious combination. Use any orange-flavoured liqueur such as Cointreau or Grand Marnier. If unavailable, add some finely grated orange zest instead.

Brown Sugar Meringue with Strawberries and Oranges

SERVES 4

Vegetable oil for oiling

3 large egg whites

175g golden caster sugar (or crushed demerara sugar)

2 oranges

300g strawberries, hulled and quartered

1tbsp orange liqueur

1tbsp icing sugar

275ml lightly whipped cream

Preheat the oven to 140°C/275°F/Gas Mark 1. Line a baking sheet with lightly oiled greaseproof paper.

Place the egg whites into a clean bowl. Whisk until they form soft peaks and you can turn the bowl upside down without them sliding out. Gradually whisk in the caster sugar, a tablespoon at a time. Now spoon the mixture on to the baking sheet, forming circles of about 8cm in diameter. Be as artistic as you like.

Place the baking sheet in the oven and cook for an hour. Then turn the oven off and leave the meringues to cool inside. Ideally, do this overnight. Store in an airtight and dry container until ready for use.

Using a sharp knife, cut away the peel and any white pith. Segment the oranges over a bowl to catch the juices. Remove any pips. Add the strawberries, liqueur and icing sugar and leave to macerate for an hour or two, covered in the fridge.

To serve, take a meringue, spoon the fruit over and top with cream.

Anyone who likes Bakewell tart will know why this tart is so delicious. You can substitute most stoned fruit for the cherries, such as apricots, peaches, nectarines, greengages and plums. Pears and quince are also good too.

Cherry and Almond Tart

SERVES 8

1 quantity Sweet Pastry (see page 155)

Flour for dusting

1tbsp cherry jam

250g cherries, stoned

3tbsp flaked almonds

For the almond paste

110g softened butter

110g caster sugar

3 eggs

1tbsp plain white flour

110g ground almonds

2tbsp Amaretto liqueur (optional)

Thinly roll out the pastry on a lightly floured board with a floured rolling pin and use to line a 23-cm tart ring that is 3cm deep, leaving a 1-cm overhang. Leave to rest for 30 minutes in the fridge. Meanwhile, preheat the oven to 190°C/375°F/Gas Mark 5. Blind bake the tart case (see page 12) for 5 minutes. Remove the tart case from the oven, remove the baking beans and paper and leave to cool slightly while you make the almond paste.

Cream the butter and sugar until pale and fluffy. Add the eggs one at a time and combine (don't worry if the mix appears to split – it will "come back" when you add the remaining ingredients). Add the flour, almonds and Amaretto, if using, and fold in. Spread the jam over the bottom of the tart case. Tip the almond paste on top and smooth the surface until level. Now push the cherries into the almond paste and scatter the almond flakes all over.

Return the tart to the oven and bake for 15 minutes. Turn the oven temperature down to 160°C/325°F/Gas Mark 3 and continue to bake for a further 20–25 minutes, or until the tip of a small knife inserted into the centre comes out clean. Return to the oven for further cooking if necessary.

Trim off the excess pastry and slide the tart on to a plate. This is best served warm with crème fraîche or thick double cream.

This is a very useful party pudding. Hazelnuts are for me, without doubt, the best nuts for chocolate. For variation, I sometimes add a few sultanas that have been soaked in rum for 48 hours.

Chocolate and Hazelnut Terrine

SERVES 10

Vegetable oil for brushing

330g best plain dark chocolate, minimum 60% cocoa solids

200g butter

Pinch of salt

135g hazelnuts, toasted, skinned and finely chopped

5 eggs, separated

65g caster sugar

Lightly brush the inside of a 25 x 8 x 7-cm terrine with oil. Line the terrine with clingfilm, leaving an overhang of 4cm on all sides. Put to one side.

Melt the chocolate, butter and salt over a pan of barely simmering water, whisking to combine. Leave in a warmish place so the chocolate becomes tepid, then fold in the hazelnuts and egg yolks.

Now, put the egg whites into a clean bowl and whisk until they form stiff peaks and you can turn the bowl upside down without them sliding out. Gradually whisk in the sugar, a tablespoon at a time. Fold one-third of the meringue into the chocolate mixture; do not completely combine. Add half of the remaining meringue and, again, mix well but not fully. Finally fold in the last bit of meringue and this time, fold thoroughly so that no trace of the egg whites remain. This three-stage folding process is designed to maximize the amount of air in the terrine.

Pour the mixture into the terrine, carefully cover with the overhanging clingfilm and refrigerate for at least 12 hours.

Unfold the clingfilm on top of the terrine. Place a rectangular serving plate on top of the terrine and invert both the plate and the terrine, giving a sharp shake halfway over – you should hear the terrine drop on to the plate. Remove the clingfilm. Slice the terrine with a hot knife and serve with a bowl of crème fraîche.

Often the simplest way is the most overlooked. It's rare to find a perfect peach these days and this is the ideal treatment. It also works for other underripe fruit such as pears, apricots and quince. For a variation, add a pinch of saffron.

Peaches and Cream

SERVES 4

1 vanilla pod
600ml water
300g caster sugar
175ml white wine
Juice of 1 lemon
1 star anise
½ cinnamon stick
4 large peaches

Using a small, sharp knife, slice the vanilla pod lengthways and scrape out the seeds. In a saucepan just large enough to hold the peaches in a single layer, place the vanilla seeds, the water, sugar, wine, lemon juice, star anise and cinnamon. Slowly bring to the boil, stirring to dissolve the sugar. Reduce the heat to low and leave to simmer for 20 minutes, without stirring. Remove the pan from the heat and put to one side to let the syrup cool.

Place the peaches in the poaching liquid and cover with a circle of greaseproof paper. Slowly bring to the boil and simmer gently for 15–20 minutes. Check by inserting a skewer – there should be a little resistance but not much. (You are aiming to undercook the peaches slightly as they will continue to soften as they cool down in the liquid.) Leave to cool, then remove the peaches from the liquid and carefully peel away the skin. Serve whole with some of the juice and a plenty of single cream.

This recipe is based on "cranachan", the traditional Scottish dessert made with raspberries and oatmeal. The flapjacks are seriously good in their own right: slightly crisp and golden on the outside, fudgy and sweet within. The recipe makes a lot but you will never be short of takers. To make your own ice cream, follow the recipe on page 150.

Raspberry, Flapjack and Vanilla Ice Cream Sundae

SERVES 4

400g raspberries

2tbsp icing sugar

1tsp lemon juice

8 scoops vanilla ice cream

2tbsp double cream, whipped

2tbsp flaked almonds, toasted (optional)

For the flapjacks

300g butter, plus extra for greasing

225g golden syrup

200g dark soft brown sugar

225g condensed milk

1tsp vanilla extract

400g oats

Pinch of salt

Preheat the oven to 190°C/375°F/Gas Mark 5. Line a rimmed baking tray (about 20cm square) with lightly buttered greaseproof paper.

To make the flapjacks, melt the butter, syrup, sugar, condensed milk and vanilla together and stir. Add the oats and salt and combine thoroughly. Spread into the baking tray – the flapjacks should be about 2cm thick. Bake the flapjacks for about 15 minutes until golden brown and firmish to the touch. Remove the tray from the oven and, using a small, sharp knife, cut the flapjacks into 4-cm squares. Leave to cool in the tray, then store them in a dry, airtight container until ready to use.

In an electric blender, process 100g of the raspberries, the icing sugar and lemon juice to make a smooth sauce. Pass the sauce through a fine sieve to remove the seeds and refrigerate until needed.

To assemble the sundaes, place a scoop of ice cream in the bottom of a tall chunky glass. Throw in a few raspberries, some of the sauce and crumble in a little flapjack. Repeat with a second layer. Top with whipped cream and lightly toasted almonds, if using.

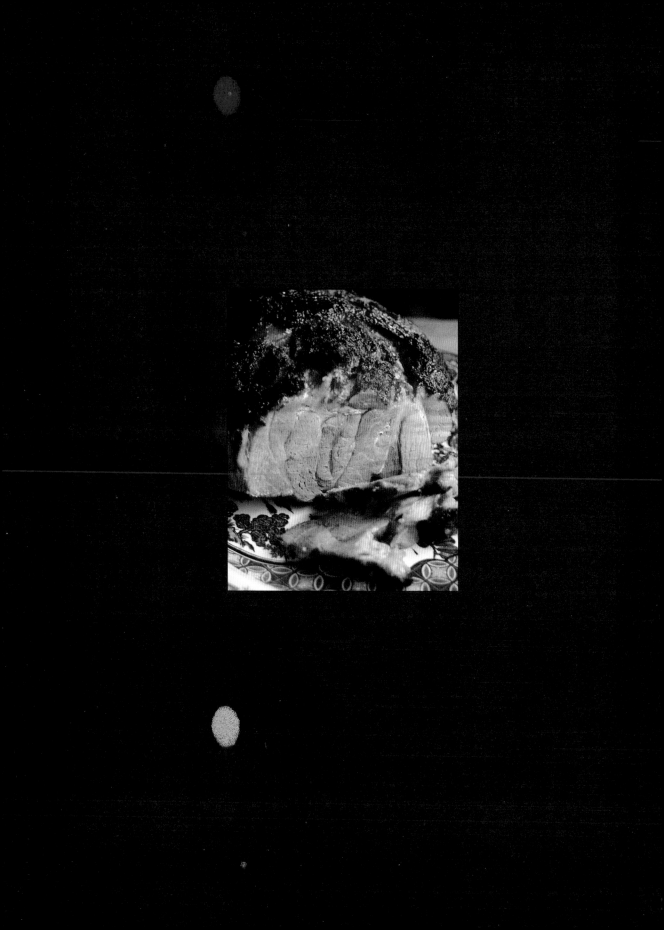

IN FROM THE COLD

It's freezing outside and you are starving as well as shivering from the cold. Whether it is a joint such as a Slow-roast Belly of Pork with Apple and Horseradish Sauce or a rich Beef and Kidney Casserole braising in the oven, nothing is more comforting than the smells wafting from the kitchen as you walk into a house. Soups, for this cook at least, are one of the most satisfying things to cook and eat. Winter is also the time for rich, warm puddings: try the Norfolk Apple and Treacle Tart, surprisingly light and moreish; or the Upside-down Pear and Ginger Cake with Vanilla Ice Cream or Crème Fraîche. Forget the waistline and indulge!

SOUPS

Light, intense and deeply satisfying, this soup is also easy to make. The amount of onions may seem alarming but they melt down to a fraction of their original volume. It doesn't matter what cider you use, but a medium-dry variety is probably best. Serve the soup with croûtes laden with melted Gruyère cheese.

White Onion and Cider Soup

SERVES 4

30g butter

1kg onions, finely sliced

2 garlic cloves, finely sliced

2tsp chopped thyme

1 bay leaf

Salt and pepper

250ml cider

1litre chicken stock

For the croûtes

1 baguette

2tbsp vegetable or olive oil,
 or 30g melted butter

Gruyère cheese, grated

In a large heavy-bottomed pan, melt the butter and add the onions, garlic, thyme and bay leaf. Season heavily with salt and pepper, turn the heat up high and cover the pan. You do not want to colour the onions in any way but you need to get the onions to wilt quickly: the combination of the salt and steam should do the trick. Check and stir if necessary during the first 5 minutes of this operation. Once the onions start to "melt", remove the lid and turn the heat down to a point where the pan is gently cooking. You now need to leave the onions to stew for at least 45 minutes to develop their sweetness: again, stir occasionally to prevent them catching on the bottom of the pan. Do not be tempted to shortcut this stage as it is key to the soup developing a full flavour.

While the onions are cooking, prepare the croûtes. Preheat the oven to 200°C/400°F/Gas Mark 6. Slice the baguette into 5-mm rounds and brush with the oil or melted butter. Place the slices on a baking sheet and bake for about 5 minutes until golden. Leave the croûtes to cool and store in a dry, airtight container (they will keep for up to a week, if necessary).

Once you are satisfied that the onions no longer have any bite to them, add the cider, stir again and turn the heat back up to full. Boil away the cider until about half of it has evaporated. Meanwhile, preheat the grill to high.

Now add the chicken stock to the pan and return to the boil. Reduce the heat and simmer for 10 minutes, then adjust the seasoning and serve. Place the croûtes on a baking tray, sprinkle with the grated Gruyère and place under the hot grill until the cheese has melted. Serve the croûtes either in the soup or on the side.

Light, clean and pretty as a picture, this soup is wonderfully fragrant and satisfying. Smoked chicken is sometimes hard to obtain, in which case use roast chicken instead for equally good results. Ideally, use fresh sweetcorn: brush with oil and char under a grill or on a ridged grill pan, then cut the kernels from the cobs. Otherwise, canned sweetcorn is fine.

Smoked Chicken and Sweetcorn Broth

SERVES 4

1 onion, finely chopped

2 garlic cloves, finely chopped

4tbsp olive oil

Salt and pepper

2tsp cumin seeds

1tsp coriander seeds

½ dried red chilli

2 small red peppers, peeled, cored and cut into 5-mm dice

75ml dry white wine

1.2litres chicken stock

200g smoked chicken, cut into 5-mm dice

1 small bunch of coriander, rinsed, leaves picked and the roots and stalks tied in a bundle

100g cooked sweetcorn kernels (see above)

Start by cooking the onion and garlic in the oil, seasoning liberally with salt and pepper. Stew over a gentle heat for at least 10 minutes. Meanwhile, dry roast the cumin and coriander seeds and dried chilli in a small frying pan over a moderate heat for about 2 minutes until you get a pleasant "roasted" aroma. Transfer the spices to a grinder or pestle and mortar and grind until fine. Put to one side.

When the onions are soft, add the red pepper and ground spices. Season with a little more salt and continue to cook over a low heat until the peppers are almost tender. Add the white wine and cook for a further 5 minutes.

Add the stock and coriander stalks to the pan and bring to the boil. Reduce the heat, add the chicken and sweetcorn and simmer for 5 minutes. Check the seasoning and adjust if necessary. Serve with a wedge of lime and chopped coriander leaves scattered over.

North African inspired, this soup is robust and filling. You can substitute any squash or pumpkin for the sweet potato, which must be one of the orange-fleshed types. This soup, served with a harissa-flavoured yoghurt, is suitable for vegetarians.

Spiced Sweet Potato and Chickpea Soup

SERVES 4

4tbsp olive oil

1 large onion, finely chopped

2 garlic cloves, finely chopped

Salt and pepper

1.2litres vegetable stock

1 leek, cut into 5-mm slices

1tbsp coriander seeds

2tsp cumin seeds

1 dried red chilli

1 bay leaf

1½tbsp tomato purée

100ml dry white wine

500g sweet potato, peeled and cut into 1-cm dice

1 red pepper, cored and cut into 1-cm dice

100g canned chickpeas, drained weight, rinsed

1 small bunch of coriander, rinsed, leaves picked and the roots and stalks tied in a bundle

For the harissa yoghurt

100g natural or Greek yoghurt

1tsp harissa

½tsp lemon juice

Heat the olive oil in a large h   ottomed saucepan and cook the onion and garlic for 10 minutes, se   them quite heavily with salt and pepper. Meanwhile, bring the   ible stock to the boil in a separate pan and season with salt. Throw in the leek and cook for 3 minutes until tender, then, using a slotted spoon, remove the leeks and leave to cool.

Meanwhile, grind the coriander and cumin seeds with the red chilli and bay leaf. The best device for this is an electric coffee grinder, but if you are feeling energetic, use a pestle and mortar. Put to one side.

When the onions have softened, add the tomato purée, stir and cook for a few minutes, then add the white wine. Cook for a further 5 minutes over a gentle heat before adding the sweet potato, the red pepper and the spice mixture. Add more salt to the newly introduced vegetables and stew for 10 minutes, then add the vegetable stock, the chickpeas and the coriander stalks.

Bring the soup to the boil, then reduce the heat and simmer until the sweet potato is tender. Remove the coriander bundle, add the cooked leeks and taste, adjusting the seasoning if necessary.

Meanwhile, combine the yoghurt, harissa and lemon juice (leave the harissa out if you think the soup is spicy enough). Serve the soup with chopped fresh coriander leaves and a swirl of the yoghurt.

This soup is light and fragrant. I am not quite sure why smoked fish and curry go together, but go together they do. We have the British Raj to thank for this particular epiphany – kedgeree must be one of the greatest dishes ever invented. Serve this soup with warm naan bread.

Curried Smoked Haddock and Lentil Soup

SERVES 4

1.2litres fish stock or water

1 small bunch of coriander, rinsed, leaves picked and the roots and stalks tied in a bundle

250g undyed smoked haddock

30g butter

1 large onion, finely chopped

1 garlic clove, finely chopped

1 bay leaf

1tbsp mild curry powder

100g potato, peeled and cut into 5-mm dice

Salt and pepper

100g canned green lentils, drained weight, rinsed

Lemon juice (optional)

Put the fish stock or water, together with the coriander roots and stalks, into a saucepan. Bring to the boil, reduce the heat and poach the haddock until it is cooked – 5 minutes should do it. Remove the fish from the liquid and leave to cool. Strain the poaching liquid and put to one side.

Melt the butter in a heavy-bottomed pan and stew the onion and garlic for at least 10 minutes. Add the bay leaf and curry powder and cook gently for a further 2 minutes, stirring all the time – the curry powder is liable to catch and burn if you are not careful.

Add the potato and season lightly with salt and pepper. Add a little of the poaching liquid, stir to amalgamate and cover with a tight-fitting lid. Cook the potatoes until tender, 20 minutes or so; if necessary add more of the liquid from time to time. Flake the smoked haddock, removing any skin and bones.

Now add the lentils and the poaching liquid and bring to the boil, then reduce the heat and simmer for 5 minutes. Drop the cooked fish into the soup with a little chopped coriander leaves. Check the seasoning and adjust if necessary, although remember the fish will be salty and it might be necessary to sharpen the soup with a little lemon juice.

This is a lovely, rich, warming winter broth with a ruby-red colour. The dried ceps add an earthiness and the bacon gives it a savoury tang, countering the sweetness of the root vegetables. I have always had better results cooking the beetroot separately, although I cannot think of any good, culinary reason why. A dollop of soured cream elevates the soup into the stuff of legends.

Beetroot, Celeriac, Cep and Bacon Soup

SERVES 4

50g dried ceps

200g bacon, cut into 1-cm dice

30g butter or lard

1 large onion, finely chopped

1 garlic clove, finely chopped

Salt and pepper

200g celeriac, peeled and cut into 5-mm dice

1 small carrot, cut into 5-mm dice

1 tsp finely chopped thyme

1 bay leaf

1.2litres chicken stock, including the cep-soaking liquid

250g cooked beetroot, peeled and cut into 5-mm dice

Soak the ceps in warm water for at least 30 minutes.

Fry the bacon in the butter or lard until lightly golden. Add the onion and garlic, season well with salt and pepper and cook gently over a low heat for 10 minutes. Meanwhile, strain the ceps and make sure that they are free from grit. If this means checking them individually, then so be it: chewing on dirt is highly disturbing. Strain the soaking liquid through muslin and add to the chicken stock.

Add the ceps, celeriac, carrot, thyme and bay leaf to the pan. Add a little more seasoning, cover with a lid and cook gently until the carrots and celeriac are tender, about 25 minutes. If necessary, add a little stock or water to prevent the vegetables from sticking. Add the diced cooked beetroot, cover with the rest of the stock and bring to the boil. Reduce the heat and simmer for 5–10 minutes to bring a coherence to the finished dish. Adjust the seasoning and serve with soured cream and chives.

"Caldo verde" is served in every bar and café in the Minho, the fertile north-west province of Portugal. It is usually a simple, rustic affair. This version is more elegant but we are still talking full-on flavours here. Use curly kale when it's available, otherwise Savoy cabbage is a good alternative. Use the raw, cooking variety of chorizo as opposed to the cured, slicing type.

Curly Kale, Potato and Chorizo Soup (Caldo Verde)

SERVES 4

150g chorizo, skinned and cut into 1-cm dice

4tbsp olive oil

1 large onion, finely chopped

1 garlic clove, finely sliced

Salt and pepper

200g potato, peeled and cut into 2-cm dice

1tsp chopped thyme

1 bay leaf

1litre chicken stock

250g curly kale, finely sliced

Extra virgin olive oil for drizzling

In a large saucepan, briskly fry the chorizo in the olive oil: this is to get the fat to run and flavour the oil. After a minute or so, remove the chorizo with a slotted spoon and put to one side. Now add the onion and garlic to the pan, season with salt and a little pepper and stew gently for at least 10 minutes, stirring from time to time to ensure the onions do not catch.

Now add the potatoes, thyme and bay leaf. Cover the pan with a lid and cook until the potatoes are tender. During this stage, it is a good idea to add a little liquid from time to time so that the potatoes steam: water or stock will do. Meanwhile, shred the kale as finely as possible. The best way to do this is to remove the hard stem and roll the leaf up tightly into a cigar shape, then slice the end into thin strands.

Once the potato is tender, remove the bay leaf, pour in the chicken stock and bring to the boil. Now, depending on your mood, either pass the soup through the coarse blade of a mouli-legumes into a clean pan, or mash the soup by hand before adding the stock. Add the kale and chorizo to the soup and simmer for about 5 minutes until the kale is perfectly tender. Adjust the seasoning and serve with a drizzle of extra virgin olive oil. Knock back a glass or two of Tio Pepe.

The quintessential winter warmer and the obvious thing to make with the ham stock retained from the Molasses-glazed Gammon (see page 131). You can substitute green split peas or red lentils for the yellow split peas. You can also use bacon instead of ham but you will need to cook it from the beginning. The mint is not essential but gives the soup a lovely freshness.

Yellow Split Pea and Ham Soup

SERVES 4

125g yellow split peas

30g butter or lard

1 garlic clove, finely chopped

1 large onion, finely chopped

1 rib of celery, finely chopped

2 small carrots, finely chopped

1tsp finely chopped thyme

1 bay leaf

Salt and pepper

1.2litres ham or chicken stock

200g cooked ham, chopped into 5-mm dice

Soak the split peas in 3 times their volume of water a few hours before you want to start the soup. This is not essential but it reduces the cooking time, which is quite long enough already.

Melt the butter or lard, add the garlic and onion and stew for at least 10 minutes or so, taking care that the onion does not colour. Add the celery, carrots, thyme, bay leaf and a decent grinding of pepper and cook gently for a further 20 minutes. Note that no salt is added at this stage.

Add the drained and rinsed split peas, cover with the stock and bring to the boil. Reduce the heat and simmer for about 90 minutes, or until the split peas have broken up. Keep a careful eye on the latter stages of cooking: the soup will begin to thicken and as it does so, the risk of catching increases.

Add the cooked ham and if you think the soup is a little thick, add more stock. Now is the time to season the soup (adding salt at the beginning prevents the split peas from cooking). Leave the salt to dissolve for a few moments and make final adjustments if necessary. Serve with finely chopped mint and chilli sherry.

TIP: A sprinkling of chilli sherry adds lift. To make this, take a bottle of medium-dry sherry – Amontillado is best – and stuff it with as many red chillies, dried or otherwise, as you think is sensible. Wait a few days before using.

STARTERS AND LUNCH DISHES

The spiciness of the curried dressing combines marvellously with the sweet parsnips – think curried parsnip soup. The green beans and lentils add texture; the poached egg, some necessary protein. Like all warm salads, this should be assembled at the last minute. The dressing can be made several days in advance and keeps almost indefinitely in the fridge.

Winter Salad of Roast Parsnips, Green Beans, Lentils, Poached Egg and Curried Dressing

SERVES 4

500g parsnips, peeled and cut into quarters lengthways

2tbsp vegetable oil

Salt and pepper

4 eggs

200g green beans, cooked, refreshed and topped and tailed

100g canned lentils, drained weight, rinsed

1 shallot, finely chopped

100g salad leaves

For the curried dressing

150ml vegetable oil

½ onion, finely chopped

1 garlic clove, finely chopped

1tbsp mild curry powder

1tbsp chopped coriander leaves (optional)

1tbsp mango chutney

1tsp Dijon mustard

Juice of 1 lime

To make the dressing, put the oil, onion and garlic into a saucepan. Cook over a gentle heat for 30 minutes, stirring occasionally. Add the curry powder and coriander and cook for 5 minutes. Tip the contents of the pan into a sturdy sieve and push the oil through with the back of a ladle. Discard the onion mixture and leave the oil to cool.

Put the mango chutney, mustard and lime juice into the bowl of a food processor. Season with salt and pepper and pulse until smooth. With the motor running, slowly add the oil in a steady stream: the dressing should end up with the consistency of pouring cream. Refrigerate until needed.

Preheat the oven to 200°C/400°F/Gas Mark 6 with a heavy-bottomed roasting tray inside. Put the parsnips, the oil and some salt and pepper into a bowl and toss the ingredients to ensure even distribution. Put the parsnips into the hot tray, return it to the oven and roast for 30 minutes. Check after 15 minutes and turn the parsnips if necessary, then return then to the oven until golden brown and juicy. Remove the parsnips from the oven and keep warm.

Poach the eggs and when you are ready to assemble the salad, place the green beans, lentils, shallot and salad leaves, into a mixing bowl. As soon as the poached eggs are ready, add the curried dressing and parsnips to the bowl and toss together. Serve immediately with a poached egg on top of each portion.

Simple to make, these fish cakes are light and very tasty. You will need a deep-fat fryer. Either serve these as part of a tapas selection with Aïoli (see page 153) and lemon, or serve them with this accompanying salad. The sweetness of the peppers goes well with the saltiness of the fritters. Piquillo peppers are canned, roasted red peppers from Spain – most good delis stock them.

Deep-fried Salt Cod Fritters with Piquillo Peppers, Green Bean and Rocket Salad

SERVES 4

225g salt cod, skinless and boneless

450g floury potatoes, peeled and cut into 2-cm dice

1 whole egg, beaten

1 egg white, beaten

1 tbsp finely chopped parsley

2 garlic cloves, grated

Salt and pepper

For the salad

6 piquillo peppers or roasted red peppers

4 tbsp Vinaigrette (see page 154)

100g rocket, rinsed and dried

100g green beans, cooked, refreshed, cooled and topped and tailed

½ shallot, sliced

To cook the salt cod from raw, soak it in a large amount of cold water 2 days before you wish to start. Change the water twice a day, making sure you rinse the fish each time. Bring a large saucepan of water to the boil and poach the salt cod until it flakes easily. It will take about 5 minutes depending on its thickness. Drain the fish and leave to cool. Skin and bone and flake the cod.

Cook the potatoes in a large pan of boiling water as if you were making mash; do not add any salt. When the potatoes are cooked, drain them well, then pass them through the coarse blade of a mouli-legumes or mash by hand. Leave the mash to cool.

Preheat a deep-fat fryer to its highest setting. Combine the flaked fish, potato, eggs, parsley and garlic. Check the seasoning, the mixture will definitely need pepper and it may well need salt, but remember the cod will be salty.

For the salad, slice the peppers and toss with the Vinaigrette and the remaining ingredients. Place on individual plates while you fry the fritters. Deep-fry the fritters by dropping tablespoonfuls of the mix directly into the hot oil and cooking until golden brown. You will need to do them in batches and the basket must be down otherwise the fritters will stick. Remove the fritters from the oil and let them sit briefly on kitchen paper to absorb any excess fat. Serve the fritters immediately with the salad, a pot of Aïoli and a wedge of lemon.

Roasting the vegetables helps bring out their full flavours. The chilli sauce accentuates the sweetness and the soured cream pulls the dish together. To make an improvised version of soured cream, add lemon juice to crème fraîche or Greek yoghurt. Use any pumpkin or squash instead of the butternut. The chilli sauce lasts forever and can be made well in advance.

Roasted Butternut and Sweet Potato Wedges, Sweet Chilli Sauce and Soured Cream

SERVES 4

500g butternut squash, peeled and cut into wedges

500g sweet potato, peeled and cut into wedges

2 garlic cloves, finely chopped

6tbsp olive oil

Salt and pepper

For the sweet chilli sauce

100ml rice wine vinegar or white wine vinegar

110g caster sugar

1tbsp Thai fish sauce

1tbsp soy sauce

1 green chilli, finely chopped

1 red chilli, finely chopped

To make the sweet chilli sauce, put the rice wine vinegar and sugar in a saucepan and bring to the boil. Reduce the heat and simmer for 20 minutes, or until it has reduced by half. Taste and check for balance. Add the fish sauce, soy sauce and chillies, stir and put aside to cool.

Preheat the oven to 200°C/400°F/Gas Mark 6 with a heavy-bottomed roasting tray inside. In a roomy bowl, combine the vegetables, garlic and oil and season generously with salt and pepper. Toss everything together to ensure even distribution of the garlic and seasoning, then place in the roasting tray and return it to the oven.

Check the vegetables after 20 minutes, when they should be starting to colour. Turn them over and return to the oven for a further 20 minutes. Once the vegetables are golden brown, check to see if they are tender (stick a knife through the thickest part: it should go in easily). If they are undercooked, turn the temperature down to prevent burning and return them to the oven.

Serve the vegetables direct from the oven with a green salad, chopped coriander and a wedge of lime. Hand round soured cream and the sweet chilli sauce separately.

Broccoli is not only delicious, it is also highly nutritious. It is an excellent source of antioxidants and vitamins. In this recipe, the anchovy dressing gives it a lovely salty tang with the chilli adding a peppery bite. Ordinary broccoli is not a bad substitute but it is worth waiting for the new season's purple-sprouting broccoli to arrive, normally, late January.

Steamed Purple Sprouting Broccoli with Red Chilli and Anchovy Dressing

SERVES 4

1.5kg purple sprouting broccoli
Salt
60g canned anchovy fillets
1½ garlic cloves, crushed
Pinch of finely chopped thyme
2tsp basil, finely chopped
2tsp Dijon mustard
2tsp red wine vinegar
3tbsp olive oil
150ml vegetable oil

To cook the broccoli, bring a large pan of heavily salted water to the boil. Separate the broccoli heads from the lower, thicker part of the stalks. Strip the leaves off the stalks and peel off any tough-looking skin. Now slice the stalks into about 5-mm thick rounds, thus allowing the stalks and heads to cook at the same rate. Put to one side.

To make the dressing, place the anchovies, garlic, herbs, mustard and vinegar into the bowl of a food processor and blitz. With the motor running, slowly add the olive oil, drop by drop and then in a steady stream until you have thick sauce resembling mayonnaise. Cover and refrigerate if not using at once.

When you are ready to serve, drop the broccoli into the water and as soon as it is tender, drain and place in a mixing bowl. Add the anchovy dressing and toss using a pair of tongs to ensure the broccoli is well coated. Serve immediately with grated Parmesan and a wedge of lemon. For a bit of crunch, consider adding some toasted flaked almonds or pine nuts if you wish.

This is a lovely vegetable pasta dish with contrasting textures, flavours and colour. The trick is to get the onions really soft and sweet – they provide the necessary counterpoint to the slight bitterness of the greens and the acidity of the tomatoes. Add a touch of red chilli if you feel like it.

Pappardelle with Winter Greens, Fontina, Onions, Cherry Tomatoes and Pecorino

SERVES 4

4tbsp extra virgin olive oil

30g butter

2 large onions, finely sliced

1 garlic clove, finely sliced

1tsp finely chopped thyme

Salt and pepper

250g winter greens, such as curly kale or Brussels sprout tops

400g pappardelle

100ml dry white wine

16 cherry vine tomatoes, rinsed and halved

150g fontina cheese, cut into 5-mm dice

Fresh basil

150g pecorino, grated

In a roomy, heavy-bottomed saucepan, melt the olive oil and butter. When hot, add the onion, garlic and thyme and season generously with salt and pepper. Let the onions stew for at least 45 minutes so that they become soft and slippery. You will need to keep a watchful eye as you do not want the onions to colour.

To prepare the greens, bring a large pan of heavily salted water to the boil. Get rid of any tough or damaged outer leaves, rinse and shred finely. In a blanching basket, cook the greens in the boiling water for 2–3 minutes until tender. Leave the greens to drain.

Meanwhile, bring another large pan of heavily salted water to the boil and add the pasta. At the same time, add the wine and tomatoes to the onions and turn the heat to high. Add a bit more salt and cook the sauce until the tomatoes start to disintegrate.

As the pasta reaches its cooking point, add the fontina, basil and greens to the sauce and give it a good stir. Drain the pasta and tip it into the sauce; if it seems a little dry, add a splash of the cooking water. Serve immediately with grated pecorino or Parmesan.

TIP: You can adapt this recipe by using different cheeses, such as dolcelatte, Taleggio and goat's cheese.

What you are looking for is fat, juicy smoked herring fillets and if you cannot get smoked herring, pickled herring will work well, as will most other smoked fish. We like to skin and slice the smoked herring before marinating it; the herring sits covered in vegetable oil for a week or two. When we are ready to use them, we drain the oil, which is then used to make the dressing.

Warm Salad of Smoked Herring, New Potatoes, Shallots and Mustard

SERVES 4

1tsp sugar

4tbsp lemon juice

Salt and pepper

4tbsp finely sliced shallot

2tsp Dijon mustard

60ml vegetable oil

1tbsp finely chopped dill

200g new potatoes, cooked peeled and sliced

25g butter

250g mixed leaves, including watercress and baby spinach

200g green beans, cooked, refreshed, cooled and topped and tailed

600g smoked herring fillets, skinned and boned

4 hard-boiled eggs, shelled and quartered

Snipped chives

Start by making the dressing. Dissolve the sugar in the lemon juice, adding a generous amount of salt and pepper. Add the shallot and mustard before slowly whisking in the oil and dill: the dressing should be sweet. This can be made well in advance and kept in the fridge.

Meanwhile, heat a large frying pan and sauté the new potatoes in the butter until golden brown; season with salt and pepper. You now need to work quickly as this salad, like all warm salads, does not like to hang around. Assemble the mixed leaves, green beans and dressing in a large bowl. Add the smoked herring to the potato pan. There should be enough residual heat in the pan and the potatoes to warm the smoked herring through, but apply more heat, if necessary.

Toss the potato and herring into the bowl. Arrange the boiled eggs and scatter with chives. Serve with wedges of lemon for squeezing over.

TIP: The best new potatoes to use for this dish are Rattes, though any waxy potato will do. Cook the potatoes with the stalks from the dill for extra flavour.

This is a delicious combination using readily available ingredients – a sort of Scotland meets Brazil. It has all you want in a dish: beautiful contrasting textures and flavours – sweet, sour, salty, hot and cold. If necessary, use salt instead of fish sauce. The salmon **must** be first class (see page 156 for suppliers). Toasted pitta bread makes an excellent substitute for the tortillas.

Smoked Salmon, Soft Flour Tortillas, Avocado Salsa, Soured Cream and Lime

SERVES 4

500g smoked salmon, sliced

Coriander leaves, to garnish

For the tortillas

7g (1 sachet) dried yeast

155ml water, blood temperature

250g strong white flour, plus extra for dusting

¾tsp salt

½tsp sugar

1tbsp olive oil

For the avocado salsa

1 ripe avocado (about 300g)

Juice of 1 lime

2tsp Thai fish sauce

1tsp caster sugar

½ red chilli, deseeded and chopped

½ green chilli, deseeded and chopped

½ garlic clove, finely chopped

1tbsp red onion, finely chopped

1 tomato, skinned, deseeded and chopped into 5-mm dice

2tbsp coriander, chopped

Salt and pepper

Start by making the tortilla dough. Dissolve the yeast in the water and leave for 5 minutes. Mix the flour, salt, sugar and olive oil together then gradually stir in the liquid. It's probably easiest to do this in a machine. Do not overprocess: you are looking for a smooth, slightly elastic dough. Add more water if it seems dry. Leave the dough in a warm place to prove, covered with a damp cloth, for about 1 hour until doubled in size.

To make the salsa, peel, stone and cut the avocado into 5-mm dice then mix the next 6 ingredients in a bowl. Leave for a good 30 minutes to allow the flavours to blend. Add the remaining ingredients and gently combine: the avocado and tomato should remain intact. Check for seasoning; it will require salt and pepper but be careful because the salmon is salty. You may need to add more lime juice – it depends on the size of the avocado.

It is desirable, if somewhat impractical, to make the tortillas to order, although they can be made in advance and reheated briefly in the oven. Whichever way you choose, you need to preheat a heavy-bottomed frying pan or better still, a ridged grill pan. Roll the dough into balls the size of a walnut. Using a floured rolling pin, roll the dough balls into thin discs on a floured surface and as you do so, throw them onto the pan. Using a pair of tongs, turn them over after a few moments and cook the other side – you want to achieve a charred and blistered effect. Once cooked, put the tortillas in a bowl covered with a tea towel, which should keep them soft.

Assemble the smoked salmon on a large platter and garnish with coriander leaves. Serve with wedges of lime and hand round the salsa, tortillas and soured cream separately.

This recipe produces a sumptuous sauce for pasta and the belt of chilli gives it a delicious kick. If you can buy authentic Italian sausage, such as a Louganica (hand-tied with string and pure meat), so much the better. Coarsely minced belly of pork works just as well, and is cheaper, too. Either way, do not attempt this recipe with ordinary sausages, no matter how good they are.

Spaghetti with Italian Sausage, Mushrooms and Red Chilli

SERVES 4

4tbsp pure olive oil

600g Italian sausage, casing removed and broken up

1 large onion, finely chopped

200g button mushrooms, sliced

1 dried red chilli, chopped

1 tsp dried oregano or herbes de Provence

1 garlic clove, finely chopped

Salt and pepper

175ml dry white wine

250ml double cream

500g dried spaghetti

Chopped parsley

Grated Parmesan cheese

In a heavy-bottomed and roomy pan, heat the olive oil and when hot, add the sausage meat and cook over a steady heat for at least 25 minutes, stirring from time to time to prevent burning. The meat should be allowed to colour, and what you are aiming for is little lumps of cooked meat as opposed to a smooth "mince" effect, which will result in a more toothsome texture. Next, add the chopped onion, the mushrooms, chilli, dried herbs, garlic and pepper to taste and stew over a moderate heat for another 25 minutes or so.

Now add the wine and as you do so, scrape up the residues that might have stuck to the bottom of the pan. Bring everything to a simmer and reduce the wine by half. Apart from a visual check, the best way to gauge this is to taste some of the liquid – there should be a slight edge to it but the "wineyness" should have gone.

Add the cream and simmer for a further 10–15 minutes until you have achieved a nice coating consistency for the pasta. Meanwhile, bring a large pan of salted water to the boil, add the spaghetti and boil until al dente. Drain well.

Adjust the seasoning of the sauce with salt. Toss the cooked pasta with the sauce, adding the parsley at the last moment. Hand the Parmesan around and serve with a green salad.

Omelettes are one of my favourite things to cook – they are the ultimate in natural, fast food. The trick is not to overbeat the eggs. In this recipe, you can substitute Gruyère, Emmental or Cheddar for the Parmesan – they all work well. I serve this with a green salad on the side.

Open Omelette of Smoked Haddock, Spring Onion, Potato, Parmesan and Crème Fraîche

SERVES ONE

3 eggs

1tsp water

Salt and pepper

Knob of butter

100g cooked undyed smoked haddock, skinned, boned and flaked

2 spring onions, stewed in a little butter

3 new potatoes, cooked, peeled and thinly sliced

1tbsp crème fraîche

4tsp grated Parmesan cheese

Preheat the grill. Lightly beat the eggs and water with a little salt and pepper. When you have everything to hand and you are ready to cook, melt the butter in a small frying pan over a high heat. Introduce the omelette mixture and immediately turn the heat down to medium. Using a spatula, lift the sides of the omelette and allow the egg to run underneath and into contact with the pan. Do not allow the omelette to take on any colour if you can help it.

When the omelette is three-quarters cooked, but with still little pools of uncooked egg on the surface, remove the pan from the heat. Working quickly, scatter the haddock, spring onions and potatoes on to the surface. Dab the crème fraîche here and there and sprinkle the Parmesan on top. Place under the grill for a couple of minutes until the surface is lightly gilded. Slide the omelette onto a plate and serve straight away.

A deluxe version of ham and cheese on toast. The bacon and cheese is nicely offset by the sweetness of the onions and tomato. Gorgonzola and cambozola are good substitutes, but Roquefort or Stilton are probably too salty to use in this recipe.

Open Sandwich of Grilled Bacon, Dolcelatte, Baby Spinach, Tomato and Roast Red Onion

SERVES 2

2 red onions, cut into 1-cm wedges

Pinch of finely chopped thyme

½ garlic clove, finely chopped

1tbsp extra virgin olive oil, plus a little extra for drizzling

6 rashers of back bacon, rind removed and grilled

4 Roast Tomatoes (see page 152), skinned

80g dolcelatte, thinly sliced

2 slices of ciabatta, cut 4cm thick

1 garlic clove, cut in half

Baby spinach leaves, rinsed, dried and lightly dressed with Vinaigrette (see page 154)

Preheat the oven to 220°C/425°F/Gas Mark 7 with a heavy-bottomed roasting tray inside. Preheat the grill to high. Put the onions, thyme, ½ chopped garlic clove and olive oil into a bowl with salt and pepper and toss thoroughly. Place the onions on the hot tray and return to the oven. They will take about 30 minutes in total to roast, but check after 15 minutes and turn the onions if necessary. They should be charred without, juicy within. Remove the onions from the oven. (The onions, once cooked, will keep in the fridge for 3 days.)

On a small baking tray, make 2 separate piles, roughly the size of your bread: start with bacon at the bottom, then the tomatoes and onions and finally the cheese. Bake in the hot oven for 4 minutes, or until the cheese has melted. Meanwhile, grill the bread on both sides. Rub some cut garlic on to one side only and drizzle with extra virgin olive oil. Pile some dressed baby spinach on to the toast. Carefully slide the bacon and cheese combo onto the spinach and serve immediately.

Carbohydrate overload you might think, but the potato adds flavour and gives a pleasing, toothsome texture to the finished dish. By all means use a different cheese: dolcelatte, Gorgonzola and fontina work well. Risottos require constant attention, so allow yourself at least 30 minutes of uninterrupted time in order to complete the dish.

Spring Onion, Potato and Taleggio Risotto

SERVES 4

750ml chicken or vegetable stock

60g butter

1 large onion, finely chopped

Salt and pepper

300g arborio rice

200g potato, peeled and cut into 1-cm cubes

2tsp finely chopped rosemary

100ml white wine

6 spring onions, trimmed and finely chopped

100g Taleggio cheese, cut into 5-mm cubes

Grated Parmesan cheese

Bring the stock to the boil and put to one side.

Melt the butter in a heavy-bottomed, roomy saucepan and add the onion. Season with salt and pepper and cook over a gentle heat for 10 minutes. Add the rice, potatoes and rosemary, coat well with the butter and cook for a further 2 minutes, stirring all the time. Add more salt and pepper.

Turn the heat up a little, add the wine, stir and simmer. When no further liquid remains, add a large ladleful of the hot stock to the pan. Continue to simmer until the rice has absorbed all the liquid. As it cooks, stir the rice more or less constantly. Repeat this process until all the remaining stock is used. Do not be tempted to add all the stock in one go – it needs to be added gradually. After 10 minutes, stir in the spring onions.

To check whether the risotto is ready, taste the rice: it should be "lava-like" in consistency and there should be no chalkiness to the bite. Stir in the Taleggio, adjust the seasoning and serve immediately. Pass the Parmesan around separately.

STEWS AND OTHER HEARTY FARE

This recipe was given to me by Mark Robinson, who runs the award-winning kitchen at The Earl Spencer in south-west London. It is a typically clever creation, which turns a normal fish pie on its head. It is utterly delicious.

Smoked Haddock Gratin with Potato, Tomato, Spinach, Crème Fraîche and Gruyère

SERVES 4

750g undyed smoked haddock

4tbsp crème fraîche

5 tomatoes, skinned and stewed in butter for 5 minutes

2tbsp chopped fresh basil

500g new potatoes, cooked, cooled, peeled and thinly sliced

250g fresh spinach, steamed, lightly squeezed and chopped

Bèchamel Sauce (see page 153), made with 400ml milk

150g grated Gruyère cheese

Preheat the oven to 220°C/425°F/Gas Mark 7.

Remove the skin and any bones from the smoked haddock. Carefully slice the haddock into thin flat slices (as per sliced smoked salmon).

Spread the crème fraîche into the bottom of a 5-cm deep pie dish. Now put in a layer of tomato, sprinkle on the basil and then add a layer of smoked haddock (use about half of it). Place the potatoes loosely on top of the fish. Scatter the cooked spinach evenly on top of the potatoes and finally use the rest of the smoked haddock as the final layer.

Cover completely with Béchamel, sprinkle the Gruyère on top and bake for 30 minutes. Leave to stand for 30 minutes before serving.

This is rich and warming. Proper home-made gnocchi should not be heavy – the trick is to cook them as soon as they have been made. The combination of the mascarpone, tomato and mint is sublime, but you can also add a little chilli if you want.

Potato Gnocchi with Slow-cooked Tomato Sauce, Mascarpone and Mint

SERVES 4

525g floury potatoes, unpeeled

75g strong white flour

2½tsp salt

Semolina flour for dusting

Salt

Butter for greasing

3 tbsp finely chopped mint

300ml Slow-cooked Tomato Sauce (see page 154)

5 tbsp mascarpone

Grated Parmesan cheese

Set a large steamer above a saucepan of boiling water and steam the potatoes in their skins until tender, about an hour. (This can be done successfully in the microwave.) Skin the potatoes as soon as they are cool enough to handle, then pass them through the finest blade of a mouli-legumes. Sift the flour, add the salt and gradually work it into the potato until you have a soft paste; take care not to overwork the mixture. You may need a little more flour depending on the moisture of the potatoes.

Divide the potato mixture into 4 portions and roll the dough into a long, even sausage shape, about 4cm in diameter. Now cut into 2–3-cm pieces and place on a tray that has been dusted with semolina flour. Repeat the process with the remaining portions of dough.

Meanwhile, preheat the grill and bring a large saucepan of salted water to the boil. Grease a gratin dish.

Drop the gnocchi into the boiling water and boil for about 2 minutes until they float to the surface, then remove them with a slotted spoon and place them directly into the gratin dish; avoid any excess water. Sprinkle the mint over the gnocchi and cover with the tomato sauce. Dab the mascarpone on top, strew with Parmesan and place under the grill until the surface of the gratin is bubbling hot and golden.

There's a bit of work involved here but let's face it, everyone loves a pie. You can substitute rabbit legs for the chicken, or add a few prunes or wild mushrooms for further variation. The filling can be made up to two days in advance. I serve this with boiled peas and mashed swede.

Chicken and Bacon Pie

SERVES 8

For the filling

6 free-range chicken legs

400g bacon

3 leeks, cut into 2-cm slices

1 onion, finely sliced

1tbsp chopped thyme

1 bay leaf

600ml chicken stock

300ml dry white wine

Salt and pepper

80g butter

7tbsp plain white flour

1 quantity of Savoury Pastry (see page 155), at room temperature

Flour for dusting

1 egg, beaten

Stage 1: put the first 8 ingredients into a large saucepan, season with salt and pepper and bring to the boil. Reduce the heat, cover with a tight-fitting lid and simmer for 40 minutes. Tip the contents of the pan into a colander underneath which you have placed a bowl to collect the juices. Transfer the chicken to a plate and leave until cool enough to handle. Set the bacon, leeks and onion aside, discarding the bay leaf. Remove the skin and pick the chicken from the bones, then break the chicken into bite-sized pieces. The liquor will produce a layer of fat from the chicken. You can skim this off and use it instead of butter in the next step.

Melt the butter in a roomy saucepan. Add the flour and mix to a paste. Gradually incorporate the reserved chicken liquid to make a thick sauce (see the method for Béchamel Sauce on page 153). Add the chicken, bacon, leek and onion and stir well. Adjust the seasoning if necessary.

Stage 2: when you are ready to bake the pie, preheat the oven to 190°C/375°F/Gas Mark 5. Divide the pastry into 2 balls, roughly two-thirds and one-third. On a lightly floured surface, roll the larger ball into a circle with a floured rolling pin and line a 20-cm tart ring, leaving a 1-cm overhang. Blind bake the case (see page 12) for 10 minutes. Remove the case from the oven and remove the baking beans and paper. Roll out the second ball slightly wider than the pie case to make a lid. Pile the chicken and bacon mix into the pie. Now dampen the rim of the pastry with the beaten egg and place the pastry lid in position on top. Press the edges together with a fork. Brush the remaining egg onto the lid. Make a small steam-hole in the centre of the pastry lid and bake the pie for 25–30 minutes, or until golden brown. Remove from the oven and trim the excess pastry from the rim with a serrated knife. Slide the pie on to a chopping board and cut into wedges.

In the ecological disaster zone that is Britain's fishing grounds, there are few fish that are not under threat. Red gurnard is abundant, firm-fleshed and tasty. There are plenty of eco-friendly alternatives – sea bream and red mullet both work well. Serve with steamed spinach and boiled new potatoes.

Baked Gurnard Wrapped in Parma Ham with Red Pepper, Fennel and Olives

SERVES 4

4 red gurnard (about 500g each), skinned, filleted and boned

Salt and pepper

8 basil leaves

8 slices of Parma ham

2 large heads of fennel

6tbsp extra virgin olive oil

1 large onion, finely chopped

2 garlic cloves, finely chopped

2 red peppers

100ml dry white wine

1tsp Pernod, or other aniseed-flavoured liqueur (optional)

75ml fish stock or water

50g Kalamata olives, stoned and sliced

Vegetable oil for frying

Seasoned plain flour for dredging

Preheat the oven to 200°C/400°F/Gas Mark 6.

Season the gurnard fillets on both sides with pepper and place 2 basil leaves along the length of each one. Wrap the fillets individually with a slice of Parma ham, then put to one side.

Prepare the fennel by chopping off the woody stalks, trimming the base and slicing into 1-cm thick wedges. (Retain the green fronds for adding later to the dish; freeze the stalks for your next fish stock.)

Heat the olive oil in a saucepan. Gently cook the onion and garlic for 10 minutes over a low heat, seasoning generously with salt and pepper. Add the fennel and red peppers to the onions and cook for a further 10 minutes. Season again. Now add the wine, Pernod, if using, fish stock and olives and simmer for a further 20 minutes. Stir in the chopped fennel fronds and keep warm.

Heat a little vegetable oil in a heavy-bottomed and roomy frying pan. Dredge the fillets in seasoned flour and fry the fish for about 1 minute on each side until golden.

Tip the fennel and red pepper stew into a shallow gratin dish and arrange the fish on top in a single layer, then cover with foil. Bake in the oven for 15 minutes.

This is a brilliant recipe that uses a huge amount of garlic. The anchovies and soy may seem a little over the top but they give the dish an amazing savouriness. If you have an aversion to anchovies – as far as I can tell, that is at least half the population – do not be put off as they are virtually indiscernible.

Pot-roast Chicken with Leeks and Anchovies

SERVES 4

Salt and pepper

2tbsp olive oil

4 large free-range chicken legs

175ml dry white wine

1kg leeks, rinsed and cut into 1-cm rounds

10 garlic cloves, lightly crushed

1tbsp chopped rosemary

50g canned anchovy fillets, finely chopped

2½tbsp light soy sauce

2tbsp finely chopped parsley

Juice of ½ lemon

Preheat the oven to 220°C/425°F/Gas Mark 7 and bring a large pan of heavily salted water to the boil.

In a heavy-bottomed frying pan, heat the olive oil and gently colour the chicken legs until they are golden brown on both sides. (A little butter added will help things along.) Transfer the chicken to a flameproof casserole large enough to hold them in a single layer. Pour the white wine into the frying pan and scrape up any residues, then add the pan juices to the chicken.

Add the leeks to the boiling water and boil for 3 minutes, then drain and add them to the casserole, together with the garlic, rosemary, anchovies and soy sauce; season generously with pepper. Put the casserole over the heat and bring the liquid to the simmer. Place the casserole in the oven with a tight-fitting lid and cook for 20 minutes. Remove the casserole from the oven and add the parsley and lemon juice. Return it to the oven for a further 10 minutes until the chicken legs are cooked through and the juices run clear when you pierce them. Taste the juices and add some salt if necessary. Serve with new potatoes and a simple dressed green salad.

An easy party dish, this is popular with vegetarians and non-vegetarians alike. The creamy saltiness of the goat's cheese goes terrifically with the sweetness of the butternut. This also freezes well, so make two and store the other. Serve with a crisp green salad on the side.

Butternut and Goat's Cheese Lasagne

SERVES 4

500g butternut squash, peeled and cut into 1.5-cm cubes

2tbsp chopped sage

2 garlic cloves, finely chopped

3tbsp extra virgin olive oil

Salt and pepper

200g dried lasagne sheets

250ml Slow-cooked Tomato Sauce (see page 154)

250g spinach, cooked, lightly squeezed and chopped

200g mild goat's cheese

400ml Béchamel Sauce (see page 153)

Grated Parmesan cheese

Preheat the oven to 220°C/425°F/Gas Mark 7 with a roasting tray inside.

Put the butternut squash, sage, garlic and olive oil into a bowl, season generously with salt and pepper and toss to distribute the ingredients evenly. Throw the squash into the hot tray and roast in the oven for 30 minutes, or until tender. Check after 15 minutes and turn the cubes if necessary. Remove the pan from the oven and put to one side.

Meanwhile, bring a large saucepan of salted water to the boil. Season with salt, add the lasagne sheets and boil for about 2–3 minutes to soften. Drain well and then tip into a bowl of cold water. Leave for 2 minutes. Remove from the cold water and lay on a clean tea towel until you are ready to assemble the lasagne.

Assemble the lasagne as follows: place about one-third of the tomato sauce in the bottom of a gratin dish. Put a layer of lasagne sheets on top. Now spread half the spinach, butternut and goat's cheese on top of the lasagne. Dab half the remaining tomato sauce on top. Repeat this procedure for the next layer. Place the third and final layer of lasagne sheets on top.

Spread the Béchamel Sauce evenly over the top and bake for 35 minutes. Remove the lasagne from the oven and sprinkle with a generous amount of grated Parmesan cheese. Return the dish to the oven and bake for a further 10–15 minutes, or until golden.

I realize pig's cheeks are a little obscure, but do try them (for a list of suppliers see page 156). They are truly delicious – succulent and full of meaty flavour. Diced shoulder or neck fillet are suitable alternatives. This is the classic bourguignon treatment.

Pig's Cheeks Braised with Red Wine, Button Onions, Mushrooms and Bacon

SERVES 4

1.2kg pig's cheeks, surface membrane removed

50g butter or lard

200g bacon, cut into 2-cm dice

1 large onion, finely chopped

2 garlic cloves, finely chopped

2tbsp plain white flour

750ml dry red wine

Salt and pepper

2 bay leaves

1tbsp chopped thyme

300g button onions, peeled

250g button mushrooms, stalks removed

Preheat the oven to 140°C/275°F/Gas Mark 1.

Ensure that the surface membrane has been removed from the pig's cheeks. If it has not, slip a sharp knife underneath the membrane and with short, jagged movements ease it off.

Melt half the butter or lard in a large, flameproof casserole over a moderate heat. Add the bacon bits and fry until they are golden, then remove them with a slotted spoon and put to one side. Turn the heat up and fry the pork – a few pieces at a time – until all sides are brown. Using a pair of tongs, transfer the meat to a plate as it browns.

When all the meat is cooked, add the chopped onion and garlic to the casserole, scrape up any residues and gently stew for 10 minutes. Now return the cheeks to the casserole, sprinkle in the flour and stir it around to soak up all the fat and juices, then gradually pour in the wine – stirring. Season heavily with salt and pepper and add the herbs. Bring to a simmer, cover with a tight-fitting lid and place in the oven for 3 hours.

Meanwhile, in a large frying pan, melt the rest of the butter and fry the button onions until they are golden; remove with a slotted spoon. Repeat the process with the mushrooms and set aside.

After 2 hours, remove the casserole from the oven. Add the button onions and mushrooms, bring the liquid back to the simmer and return the casserole to the oven for the final hour. Taste and adjust the seasoning if necessary.

These creamy lentils are wonderful with almost anything, but they are particularly good with pork and chicken. They also go well with most fish. You can change the base notes by adding dried mushrooms or by using different herbs such as mint and rosemary.

Calf's Liver with Creamed Lentils, Mustard and Bacon

SERVES 4

150g Puy lentils or 300g cooked, lentils (drained weight)

Salt and pepper

40g butter

200g bacon, cut into 1-cm cubes

1 onion, finely choppd

2 garlic cloves, finely chopped

½ rib of celery, finely chopped

1 leek, rinsed and cut into 2-cm slices

1 bay leaf

1tbsp chopped thyme

175ml dry white wine

175ml chicken stock

175ml double cream

1½tbsp Dijon mustard

800g calf's liver, thinly sliced

Vegetable oil

2tbsp finely chopped sage

Put the lentils into a saucepan, cover with double their volume of cold water and bring to the boil. Reduce the heat and simmer for about 40 minutes until tender. Remove the pan from the heat and season the lentils with salt, then put to one side.

In a heavy-bottomed saucepan, melt the butter and fry the bacon until golden on all sides. Add the onion and garlic, season with salt and pepper and scrape up any residues that may have stuck to the pan. Stew for 10 minutes, stirring occasionally, before adding the celery, leek, bay leaf and thyme. Season again, stir and stew for a further 20 minutes over a low heat.

Add the wine, bring to the boil and boil until the wine has reduced by half. Add the chicken stock and cream and return to the boil, then reduce the heat and simmer for 25 minutes, or until the liquid is thick and creamy. Add the drained lentils and the Dijon mustard to the pan, bring back to the boil and then turn off the heat.

Heat a large, heavy-bottomed frying pan or ridged grill pan until it is red hot. Brush the slices of liver with a little oil, season with salt and pepper and press the sage gently on to both sides. Place on to the pan for 1 minute each side and serve immediately with the lentils and some form of greenery.

My agent, Michael Halden, insisted that this recipe be included – it's one of his favourites. If your budget allows, buy the English grey-legged partridge for its superior, gamey flavour, rather than its farmed, red-legged cousin. Serve with Bread Sauce (see page 155). The cabbage can be made in advance and reheated. I serve this with game chips or roast vegetables.

Roast Partridge, Savoy Cabbage and Bread Sauce

SERVES 4

4 partridge, gutted and trussed

Vegetable oil for brushing

80g butter

Salt and pepper

For the Savoy cabbage

30g butter or duck fat

100g smoked bacon, cut into
  1-cm dice

1 onion, finely sliced

1 garlic clove, finely sliced

½ rib of celery, finely chopped

½tsp chopped thyme

1 bay leaf

2 carrots, cut into 5-mm dice

1 small Savoy cabbage, cored and
  shredded into 1-cm strips

100ml chicken stock

Start with the Savoy cabbage. Melt the butter or fat in a roomy, heavy-bottomed saucepan. When hot, add the bacon and cook gently for about 10 minutes until it is well coloured.

Add the next 5 ingredients and season lightly with salt and pepper. Scrape up any residues that have stuck to the bottom of the pan and cook for a further 10 minutes. Add the carrots and cook for another 5 minutes. Throw in the cabbage and season well again. Add the chicken stock and give everything a good stir.

Cover and cook over a moderate heat for about 5 minutes until the cabbage is tender, but still retaining its vibrancy. Keep warm if using immediately or leave to cool if you are reheating for later use.

Meanwhile, preheat the oven to its highest setting. Heat a large, ovenproof frying pan or roasting tray over a high heat. Rub a little oil over the birds and season with salt and pepper (the oil helps the seasoning to stay on).

Melt the butter in the pan over a high heat, then brown each breast for about 3 minutes until golden. Now place the birds breast-side up into the pan and place in the oven for 15 minutes basting after 7 minutes. Remove the pan from the oven and leave the partridge to rest for 15 minutes in a warm place until ready to serve.

After the birds have rested, tip any juices that may have collected in their cavities into the Savoy cabbage. There should be sufficient moisture in the cabbage not to warrant a gravy. Serve with game chips or roast vegetables and bread sauce.

This is a fabulous winter warmer, one of our vegetarian top sellers. The beans to use are black turtle beans, not the Chinese fermented variety. The beans need to be soaked for 24 hours prior to using. (Canned kidney beans are an okay substitute.) This is better made a day ahead and reheated. If you have any leftover chilli, it goes well with grilled chicken.

Black Bean Chilli with Coriander and Soured Cream

SERVES 4

200g dried black turtle beans

1 bunch of coriander, leaves picked and roots and stalks tied in a bundle

Pinch of bicarbonate of soda (optional)

Salt and pepper

5tbsp olive oil

1 onion, finely chopped

4 garlic cloves, finely chopped

2 green peppers (about 250g), cored and cut into 2-cm pieces

2 red peppers, (about 250g) cored and cut into 2-cm pieces

1 green chilli, deseeded and finely chopped

1 red chilli, deseeded and finely chopped

1tbsp cumin seeds

1tbsp coriander seeds

1tsp allspice berries

2.5cm piece of cinnamon stick

1 bay leaf

400g canned chopped tomatoes

Soak the beans in 3 times their volume of water for 24–48 hours, then drain and rinse well.

Throw the drained beans and the coriander stalks into a large pot, cover with cold water at least 5cm above the beans and bring to the boil. Add a pinch of bicarbonate of soda, reduce the heat and simmer for about 1½–2 hours until the beans are tender. Remove the pot from the heat, season with salt and stir.

In a heavy-bottomed saucepan, heat the olive oil. Add the onion and garlic, season well and fry for 10 minutes over a low heat. Add the peppers and the chillies and cook for a further 15 minutes, then season again.

Grind the cumin, coriander and allspice in a grinder. Add the ground spices, cinnamon, bay leaf and tomatoes to the pan, give everything a good stir and bring to the boil. Reduce the heat and simmer for 25–30 minutes (or until the peppers are tender), then add the drained beans – retaining some of the cooking liquid in case the chilli needs loosening later on. Bring the chilli back to a simmer and cook for a further 5 minutes. Adjust the seasoning and serve sprinkled with copious amounts of chopped coriander and soured cream for spooning over.

Most people who do not like kidneys still seem to love a bit of Kate and Sidney – one of life's little paradoxes. My preferred ratio is three parts steak to one part kidney. Be careful not to buy veal kidneys: they are delicious but ruinously expensive. Serve with boiled potatoes and creamed horseradish on the side.

Beef and Kidney Casserole with Creamed Horseradish

SERVES 4

50g butter or lard

900g chuck steak, cut into 4-cm cubes

300g ox kidneys, skinned and cut into 4-cm cube

1 large onion, finely sliced

2 garlic cloves, finely sliced

2 carrots, chopped into large chunks

1 rib of celery, finely sliced

200g field mushrooms, cut into 2-cm chunks

2tsp chopped thyme

2 bay leaves

3tbsp plain white flour

400ml red wine

200ml beef or chicken stock

Salt and pepper

Chopped parsley

For the creamed horseradish

4tbsp crème fraîche

½tsp sugar

1tbsp lemon juice

1tsp English or Dijon mustard

4tbsp freshly grated horseradish

Preheat the oven to 140°C/275°F/Gas Mark 1.

Melt the butter or lard in a flameproof casserole. When hot, fry the beef, a few pieces at a time, until it is golden brown all over. Using tongs, transfer the meat to a plate. Repeat the process for the kidneys.

Now add the vegetables and herbs, season well with salt and pepper and stir around for 5 minutes, scraping up any residues as the vegetables release their juices.

Return the meat to the pot, sprinkle in the flour, stir it around to soak up the fat and then gradually pour in the wine and stock. Bring the liquid to the boil, then cover with a tight-fitting lid and place the casserole in the oven for 2½ hours.

Meanwhile, to make the creamed horseradish, combine all the ingredients in a mixing bowl and season with salt and pepper. Cover and chill until required.

Remove the casserole from the oven and adjust the seasoning if necessary. Strew with chopped parsley and serve.

This sweet mustard glaze transforms gammon into something special. Serve hot with mash, greens and the cider juices from the pan. Use the leftovers in pies, sandwiches and soup.

Molasses-glazed Gammon

SERVES 12–16

3–4kg gammon, boned and rolled

5 carrots, finely chopped

3 onions, finely sliced

3 garlic cloves, finely sliced

4 ribs of celery, finely chopped

4 leek tops, rinsed and
finely chopped

3 bay leaves

20 black peppercorns

4 thyme sprigs

4 star anise

For the molasses glaze

4tbsp Dijon mustard

6tbsp soft dark brown sugar

200ml medium cider or apple juice

Put the gammon into a large pan and cover with water. Cover with a tight-fitting lid, bring to the boil, then discard the water. Now add the remaining ingredients, cover with fresh water and simmer for 75 minutes.

Meanwhile, after an hour, preheat the oven to its highest setting. Remove the gammon from the pan, place in a roasting tray and leave to cool for a few minutes. Continue to boil the cooking liquid until it has reduced by half, then strain and discard the vegetables. (It is now strong enough to use for soups and stews. Cool and freeze for later use if necessary.)

Remove the string from the gammon and carefully cut off the skin, leaving as much fat as possible. The skin should come away quite easily, although it is a little tricky because the gammon is still hot. Score the gammon by making shallow criss-cross cuts, each about 1cm apart. Avoid cutting too deeply into the flesh, although it doesn't matter if you do.

Using a flat-bladed knife or spatula, smear the mustard for the glaze all over the exposed fat. Now for the messy bit: take a spoonful of the sugar at a time and use your fingers to pat it onto the mustard. When the gammon is completely covered, pour the cider or apple juice into the pan.

Place the gammon, fat side uppermost, into the oven and bake for a further 45 minutes, basting it every 10 minutes with the cider and juices.

Remove the gammon from the oven and keep warm. To make a quick sauce, pour some of the ham stock into the roasting tray, scraping up any residual bits and pieces. Simmer for a few moments and taste. Add a little more mustard if necessary, then strain into a jug.

The Apple and Horseradish Sauce (see page 154) is a recipe direct from Simon Hopkinson's **Independent** food column. The horseradish gives the apple a lovely smokiness, which goes brilliantly with the pork. Allow 2 hours cooking time for the pork with a further 30 minutes for resting.

Slow-roast Belly of Pork, Red Cabbage, Apple and Horseradish Sauce

SERVES 8-10

1 belly of pork (4–5kg)

2tbsp vegetable oil

Salt and pepper

For the red cabbage

1 red cabbage (about 1.2kg)

2tbsp butter, dripping or duck fat

1 large onion, finely sliced

2 garlic cloves, finely sliced

2 bay leaves

2 star anise

1 cinnamon stick, broken into 3 pieces

3tbsp red wine vinegar

3tbsp caster sugar

Preheat the oven to its highest setting with a heavy-bottomed roasting tray inside. Lightly score the skin of the pork belly by making shallow parallel incisions along the width of the belly. For ease of carving, the cuts should be 2–3mm apart. Lightly oil both sides of the joint and season heavily with salt and pepper (pork loves pepper). Remove the roasting tray from the oven and place the belly skin-side down. Immediately return to the oven and roast for 25 minutes. Take the pork out of the oven. Reduce the oven temperature to 160°C/325°F/Gas Mark 3. Turn the joint over so the skin side is now uppermost and roast for a further 90 minutes. Check the pork after 80 minutes and if the crackling looks iffy, turn the oven up to maximum and give it a quick blast.

Remove the pork and leave to rest for at least 25 minutes by which time some useful porky juices will have accumulated (add these to the red cabbage). To carve, remove the row of ribs (you should be able to pull them out) and carve thickly.

Meanwhile, quarter the red cabbage and discard any damaged outer leaves. Slice the cabbage into thin strips cutting across the grain; discarding the white core. In a heavy-bottomed saucepan, melt the butter or fat. Add the onion, garlic, bay, star anise and cinnamon and fry over a brisk heat for 10 minutes. Season and stir occasionally to avoid colouring the onion. Add the cabbage, season and stir. Cook for a further 5 minutes. Add the vinegar, stir and turn the heat down so that the cabbage wilts. Partially cover and cook for 25 minutes, stirring occasionally. Add the sugar and cook for 30 minutes, or until the cabbage is tender. Serve with the pork and Apple and Horseradish Sauce.

Economical, easy and scrumptious, this is a great one-pot dish. Use shoulder of lamb if mid-necks are unavailable. The combination of the sherry, cinnamon and peppers gives this dish a delicious aromatic sweetness and warmth. Serve with green beans. The potatoes I use for this dish are Desirées, also known as "reds".

Mid-neck Fillet of Lamb with Potatoes, Pearl Barley, Red Pepper and Sherry

SERVES 4–6

2tbsp vegetable oil

1.2kg mid-neck fillet of lamb, cut into 3-cm chunks

2 onions, finely chopped

4 garlic cloves, finely sliced

1 bay leaf

1 cinnamon stick, about 7.5cm, broken into 2 pieces

2tsp ground ginger

150ml dry sherry

450ml chicken stock or water

3tbsp pearl barley

3 red peppers, cored and cut into 2-cm squares

650g potato, peeled and cut into 2-cm cubes

Juice of ½ lemon

Salt and pepper

Medium-dry sherry, to serve

Preheat the oven to 150°C/300°F/Gas Mark 2.

Heat a large, flameproof casserole over a high heat for 5 minutes. Add the oil and fry the lamb until golden brown on all sides, cooking in batches if necessary. Transfer the lamb to a plate. Now fry the onions and garlic until well-coloured (about 10 minutes), scraping up any meaty residues. Add the remaining ingredients and season generously with salt and pepper. Bring to the boil, cover with a tight-fitting lid and place in the middle of the oven for about 2 hours.

Remove the casserole from the oven. Stir in the lemon juice. Taste the sauce and adjust the seasoning if necessary. Sprinkle with sherry and serve with green beans on the side.

WINTER PUDDINGS

This is delicious served with crème fraîche or whipped cream. If you are feeling creative, serve with some home-made ginger ice cream or add a little ginger syrup to the cream.

Upside-down Pear and Ginger Cake

SERVES 8–10

100g butter, plus extra for greasing

200g caster sugar

4 eggs, separated

200g plain white flour

2tsp baking powder

1tsp ground ginger

1tsp ground cinnamon

Pinch of salt

For the pear base

100g butter

4 large, firm pears, peeled, cored and cut into 1-cm slices

1tbsp lemon juice

180g caster sugar

50g stem ginger, finely chopped

2tbsp ginger syrup from the stem ginger

Preheat the oven to 180°C/350°F/Gas Mark 4. Line the sides and bottom of a 23-cm springform cake tin with buttered greaseproof paper.

To make the pear base, melt the butter in a heavy-bottomed frying pan over a moderate heat. Toss the pears and lemon juice in a bowl, then add to the butter and cook gently for about 3 minutes depending on the ripeness of the fruit. Add the sugar, ginger and syrup and cook for a further 4 minutes, stirring to dissolve the sugar. Remove the pears with a slotted spoon and arrange in the bottom of the cake tin. Turn up the heat under the frying pan and boil the remaining liquid for another 5 minutes until a light caramel starts to form. Pour the caramel over the pears and put to one side.

To make the cake, cream the butter and sugar until light and fluffy. Add the egg yolks one at a time, beating after each addition. Sift the flour, baking powder, spices and salt over, then gently fold in. Beat the egg whites in a clean bowl until stiff peaks form. Fold the egg whites into the cake mixture with a large metal spoon or spatula.

Pour the mixture over the pears and smooth the surface. Bake the cake for 40 minutes on the middle shelf of the oven until a skewer inserted into the centre comes out clean. Remove the cake from the oven and leave it in its tin for 5 minutes before inverting on to a plate. Unclip and remove the tin and serve the cake warm.

A terrifically easy, foolproof recipe, this is just the thing for those overripe bananas you've been meaning to eat for the past week. Serve this with vanilla ice cream, crème fraîche or whipped cream. Both parts of this recipe can be made well in advance and they freeze for future use.

Toasted Banana Bread with Butterscotch Sauce

MAKES 1 LOAF (ENOUGH FOR 10)

For the banana bread

200g soft butter, softened, plus a little extra for greasing

225g dark muscavado sugar

3 eggs, beaten

2 ripe bananas, mashed roughly

55g walnuts, roughly chopped

90g sultanas

90g white self-raising flour

90g plain white flour

1tsp bicarbonate of soda

For the butterscotch sauce

125g soft brown sugar

125g butter, cut into small pieces

125ml double cream

Splash of whisky or brandy

Preheat the oven to 180°C/350°F/Gas Mark 4. Lightly grease a 25 x12 x 7-cm bread tin, then line the bottom with buttered greaseproof paper.

Using an electric mixer, cream the butter and sugar until it is smooth and pale. Using a large spoon or spatula, fold in the eggs, bananas, walnuts and sultanas. Sift both flours and the bicarbonate of soda over the surface and fold into the other ingredients.

Transfer the mixture into the bread tin and smooth over the surface. Bake for 50 minutes on the middle shelf of the oven until a clean skewer inserted into the middle comes out clean. Remove the tin from the oven, turn out the banana bread and leave to cool on a wire rack.

To make the butterscotch sauce, place all the ingredients in a small pan and boil for 5 minutes, stirring, until completely smooth. Meanwhile, preheat the grill to high.

To assemble the dish, cut the bread into 1.5-cm slices and toast both sides under the hot grill. Place the toasted banana bread on the middle of a plate, pour the sauce on top and add a scoop or two of ice cream.

This recipe was inspired by a similar dish in Elizabeth Kent's **Country Cuisine**; a 1970s paperback I misappropriated from my mum. We have produced this tart more or less constantly over the years and it has been hugely popular with our customers. Moist, rich and crumbly, this is best served warm with a jug of thick cream.

Norfolk Apple and Treacle Tart

SERVES 8

1 quantity Sweet Pastry (see page 155)

Flour for dusting

1 large Bramley cooking apple

4 slices of white bread, crusts removed and breadcrumbed

8tbsp golden syrup

Juice of 2 lemons and the finely grated rind of 1

2 eggs, lightly beaten

150ml double cream

Preheat the oven to 190°C/375°F/Gas Mark 5. Thinly roll out the pastry on a lightly floured board, using a floured rolling pin and use to line a 23-cm tart ring, leaving a 1-cm overhang. Leave to rest for 30 minutes in the fridge. Blind bake the tart case (see page 12) for 10 minutes. Remove the tart case from the oven and increase the oven temperature to 200°C/400°F/Gas Mark 6. Remove the baking beans and paper from the tart case and put the tart case to one side.

Meanwhile, grate the apple coarsely and mix with the breadcrumbs in a large bowl. Heat the syrup to lukewarm and stir it into the breadcrumbs with the lemon zest and juice, eggs and cream. When all the ingredients are well blended, pour into the tart case and bake for 10 minutes. Reduce the oven temperature to 180°C/350°F/Gas Mark 4 and bake for a further 20–25 minutes until the filling is slightly wobbly to the touch and just set.

Remove the tart from the oven and trim off the excess pastry. Transfer to a plate and serve warm.

Lovely and moist with the apricots providing necessary texture. The poaching recipe for the apricots works equally well for pears, peaches, nectarines and quince. Once refrigerated, the apricots will last indefinitely and are also great with Greek yoghurt and shortbread. Just remember you have to begin the poached apricots a day ahead. You will need a 20 x 24 x 6-cm cake tin .

Carrot Cake with Apricots and Lemon Fromage Frais

SERVES 8

butter for greasing

4 eggs

350g caster sugar

115ml vegetable oil

225g carrots, coarsely grated

125g canned, crushed pineapple, drained weight

450g plain white flour

2tsp baking powder

½tsp grated nutmeg

1½tsp bicarbonate of soda

½tsp ground mixed spice

1tsp ground cinnamon

110g chopped walnuts

For the poached apricots

225g dried apricots

300ml water or poaching liquid

150g caster sugar

115ml white wine

½ vanilla pod, split in half

Juice of ½ lemon

½ star anise

For the lemon fromage frais

500g fromage frais or Greek yoghurt

finely grated rind of 2 lemons

1tbsp icing sugar

To make the poached apricots, soak the apricots in cold water for 8 hours, or overnight; drain the apricots. Combine the remaining ingredients in a roomy saucepan and bring to the boil. Add the apricots to the poaching liquid, cover with a circle of greaseproof paper and simmer for 15 minutes until tender; put aside to cool.

Preheat the oven to 190°C/375°F/Gas Mark 5 and line the bottom and sides of a 20 x 24 x 6 cm (approximate) square cake tin with buttered greaseproof paper. Blend the eggs and sugar in a food processor, then pour in the oil in a slow, steady stream. Transfer the mixture to a bowl and fold in the carrots and pineapple. Add the remaining ingredients and combine well. Tip the cake mixture into the cake tin and bake on the middle shelf of the oven for about 45 minutes, or until a skewer into the middle of the cake comes out clean. Transfer to a wire rack and leave the cake to cool.

Meanwhile, to make the fromage frais, combine the fromage frais or yoghurt, lemon zest and sugar in a mixing bowl. Serve the cake with a few of the apricots and syrup together with a spoonful or two of the fromage frais.

TIP: don't buy ready-to-eat dried apricots.

This cheesecake does not need to be baked, although it should be made at least 12 hours in advance to give it time to set. A tablespoon of Cognac added to the chocolate will do it no harm. You can also brush some melted chocolate on to the biscuit base, which gives it an interesting crunch. Serve with a little chocolate sauce.

Chocolate and Mascarpone Cheesecake

SERVES 8–10

280g plain dark chocolate, chopped, plus extra to decorate, if desired

Pinch of salt

5 eggs, separated

90g caster sugar

310g mascarpone or cream cheese

90ml double cream, lightly beaten until floppy but not thick

For the base

200g digestive biscuits, crushed

100g butter, melted

75g hazelnuts, toasted and finely chopped

Line the bottom and sides of a 23-cm springform cake tin with greaseproof paper.

To make the base, mix the biscuits with the butter and hazelnuts, then lightly press over the bottom of the cake tin. Smooth the surface so the crumbs are concave rather than level and thicker on the outside. Place in the fridge for 30 minutes to firm up.

Meanwhile, melt the chocolate in a heatproof bowl set over a saucepan of barely simmering water with a pinch of salt. When the chocolate has melted, remove it from the heat and leave it to cool slightly.

Place the egg yolks and sugar in another mixing bowl and place this over the pan of simmering water. Now, using an electric hand whisk, beat the mixture for about 10 minutes until it becomes thick and creamy. It should at least double in volume. Put aside to cool.

Beat the mascarpone or cream cheese and add it to the chocolate. Gently fold the egg mixture into the chocolate, but do not mix it in completely. Whisk the egg whites to the soft peak stage and carefully fold them into the chocolate mix. Finally fold in the whipped cream.

Now pour the chocolate mixture into the cake tin and smooth the surface. Cover and chill for at least 5 hours. Decorate with grated chocolate, if you wish.

Stunning to look at, light and refreshing, this is the perfect way to finish a heavy meal. If you do not care for the aniseed flavour of Ricard, you can leave it out; however, it is well worth trying as the aniseed does provide an intriguing, barely discernable taste that is lovely.

Blood Orange and Mint Jelly

SERVES 4

3 gelatine leaves

6 blood oranges

400ml freshly squeezed blood orange juice

90g caster sugar

1½tbsp chopped mint

1tsp Ricard or Pernod (optional)

Put the gelatine leaves in a small bowl of cold water to soften. Using a small, serrated knife, segment the oranges, cutting off the peel and the whole pith. Working over a bowl to catch the juice, separate the segments by cutting down either side of the membrane. Remove any pips and place the segments in a shallow, glass serving bowl. If this sounds like too much trouble, slice the oranges instead.

Strain the juice through a fine sieve. Put it into a small saucepan over a low heat, add the sugar and stir to dissolve. Add the mint and Ricard, if using. Remove the gelatine from the water and give it a good squeeze. Add it to the warm orange juice and, using a whisk, whisk to dissolve it thoroughly. Leave to cool to blood temperature and pour over the oranges. Cover and refrigerate the jelly until set.

A fresh take on the rhubarb-and-custard theme. The tart is just delicious with a consistency similar to a crème brûlée. It is not terribly sweet so you need to ensure the rhubarb has plenty of sugar. The tart needs to be eaten on the day it is made.

Cream Tart with Stewed Rhubarb and Orange

SERVES 8

1 quantity Sweet Pastry (see page 155), at room temperature

Flour for dusting

4 egg yolks

1tbsp caster sugar

600ml double cream

2tbsp Armagnac or brandy

Seeds of 1 vanilla pod

Freshly grated nutmeg

For the stewed rhubarb

1 orange

900g rhubarb, cut into 3-cm slices

200g soft brown sugar

1 vanilla pod (from the tart)

1 star anise, broken into a few pieces

1tsp ground ginger

Preheat the oven to 190°C/375°F/Gas Mark 5.

Thinly roll out the pastry on a lightly floured board, using a floured rolling pin and use to line a 23-cm tart ring, leaving a 1-cm overhang. Leave to rest for 30 minutes in the fridge. Blind bake the tart case (see page 12) for 10 minutes. Remove the baking beans and paper and return the tart case to the oven for a further 10–15 minutes, or until lightly golden brown. Remove the tart case from the oven and set aside to cool. Reduce the oven temperature to 150°C/300°F/Gas Mark 2.

Beat the egg yolks, sugar, cream, Armagnac or brandy, and vanilla seeds together and pour into the tart case. Sprinkle a little nutmeg over the surface. Carefully place the tart back in the oven and bake for a further 40 minutes until the filling has set: it should still be slightly wobbly in the centre. Leave the tart to cool in the tin or on a wire rack and trim the excess pastry from the rim.

Meanwhile, to make the rhubarb, use a vegetable peeler to cut 4 strips of peel from the orange. Using a sharp knife, remove any pith that is still attached to the peel and squeeze the orange juice. Now put all of the ingredients into a mixing bowl and toss to ensure even distribution. Transfer to an ovenproof dish, cover loosely with foil and bake on the bottom shelf of the oven for 30 minutes until a sharp knife inserted into the thickest piece doesn't meet with any resistance. Remove the tart from the oven and leave to cool on a wire rack. This is best served at room temperature.

SIDE DISHES & BASIC RECIPES

SIDE DISHES

Chips

SERVES 4

1kg Maris Piper potatoes, peeled
Salt

We are famous at The Havelock for our chips. A good chip should be lightly golden and crunchy on the outside and fluffy within. There are many good chip-making potatoes but best of all is the Maris Piper, lovingly known in the trade as the "chipper's friend".

Cut the potato into your preferred style of chip. Place the chips into a bowl and soak in water ideally for 12 hours or longer. Preheat your deep-fat fryer to 130°C/266°F. Drain the chips into a colander and examine the bottom of the bowl for signs of starch – no starch is bad, lots is good. Now rinse the chips by pouring large amounts of water over them, then pat dry. Fry the chips in batches taking care not to overfill the basket. The chips are cooked when they are soft – give one a squeeze between your thumb and forefinger. The chips should not be allowed to take on a colour. Stage one is now complete and the chips should be left to cool. They will keep well in the fridge for anything up to 3 days. In fact, they are noticeably better made a day or two in advance. To serve the chips, move on to stage 2. Preheat your fryer to maximum, usually 190°C/375°F. Deep-fry the chips to the desired colour and place them in a bowl lined with absorbent kitchen paper. Toss with salt and serve immediately with a nice bowl of Aïoli (see page 153).

Proper Mashed Potato

SERVES 4

1.5kg potatoes, peeled and cut into 3-cm cubes
3 garlic cloves, peeled, but left whole (optional)
Salt and white pepper
50g butter
100ml double cream
50ml milk

I think the key to a really good-tasting mash is lots of white pepper. The choice of potato is up to you: red-skinned Desirées and Marfonas are both excellent.

Leave the potatoes to soak in water to cover, preferably for 12 hours or longer, then tip them into a colander and rinse.
Place the potatoes in a pan and cover with cold water. Add the garlic, if you are using, and plenty of salt and bring to the boil.
Meanwhile, slowly melt the butter in the cream and milk. Add plenty of white pepper and put aside. Check the potatoes are tender and then drain. Shake off the excess water and then mash as quickly as possible. Beat in the milk, cream and butter and adjust the seasoning, if necessary.

Boulangère Potatoes

SERVES 4

50g butter

1.5kg potatoes, either peeled or unpeeled

400g onions, finely sliced

2 garlic cloves, finely sliced

2 bay leaves, torn into small pieces

200ml chicken stock

Good enough to eat on their own, these potatoes go well with any roasted red meat, particularly roast lamb. There are many ways to vary the dish: use cooked streaky bacon or cheese for added savouriness – or different herbs, such as rosemary or sage.

Preheat the oven to 200°C/400°F/Gas Mark 6. Use a small amount of the butter to lightly grease a gratin dish. Decide what to do with the potatoes. Leaving them unpeeled lends a more rustic effect (and no doubt better for you nutritionally) in which case rigorously scrub the potatoes clean – otherwise peel. Finely slice the potatoes using a mandolin or a large, sharp knife. Place a layer of potato in the bottom of the dish followed by a layer of onion and the odd piece of bay leaf and garlic, seasoning each layer generously with salt and pepper. Continue the layering process until you end up with a top layer of potato. Pour the stock over and dot the surface with the remaining butter. Bake the potatoes for about an hour or so until golden brown and if you insert a sharp knife into the centre, there is little or no resistance. If you wrap the dish in foil, it will keep quite well in a warm place for 30 minutes.

Creamed Leeks and Mint

SERVES 4

6 large leeks, green part removed

30g butter

Salt and pepper

125ml dry white wine

200ml double cream

4 tbsp chopped mint

An old favourite. This goes well with most dishes, particularly roasts. The important element is the white wine, which gives the dish its balance. You can substitute other herbs for the mint – rosemary is especially good.

Prepare the leeks by discarding the tough outer layer and slice them in half lengthways, then chop into 3-cm pieces and rinse well. Drain the leeks in a colander, giving it a good shake to remove the excess water. Melt the butter in a heavy-bottomed saucepan and add the leeks. Season with salt and pepper and stew gently until almost tender, probably 10 minutes or so. Add the white wine and boil vigorously until reduced by at least half. Pour in the cream and simmer for a further 10 minutes, stirring from time to time to prevent the leeks from sticking. At the last moment, add the mint, then serve. Note: if you are using the more robust herbs, such as rosemary or sage, they should be added at the same time as the leeks.

Jerusalem Artichoke Gratin

SERVES 4

50g butter, plus a little extra for greasing

Juice of ½ lemon

700g Jerusalem artichokes, peeled

800g potatos, peeled

250ml double cream

250ml milk

2 garlic cloves, finely sliced

1tsp chopped thyme or rosemary

Salt and pepper

This dish is a variation on a potato dauphinoise and goes well with many roast and grilled meats, particularly duck. It's a useful recipe to know as it can be adapted to most root vegetables, such as celeriac, swede and turnip. They all work well.

Peeling the artichokes always takes a bit of time so do it in advance. They discolour quickly once peeled, so place them in a bowl of cold water into which you have added the juice of half a lemon. They can be kept like this for up to 2 days if stored in the fridge. Meanwhile, preheat the oven to 200°C/400°F/Gas Mark 6 and grease a gratin dish. In a roomy saucepan that will accommodate all the ingredients, bring the cream, milk, garlic and thyme to the boil, then reduce the heat and simmer for 10 minutes. Turn off the heat. Meanwhile, using a mandolin or alternatively, a large, sharp knife, thinly slice the potato and artichokes and drop them into the saucepan. Now, gently combine everything, adding copious quantities of salt and pepper to taste. Tip everything into the gratin dish and rearrange the slices so the surface is reasonably level. Dot with the remaining butter and bake for an hour or so until a small sharp knife inserted into the centre meets little or no resistance. Covered with foil, this will keep well for up to 30 minutes in a warm place.

Steamed Greens, Red Chilli, Oyster Sauce and Garlic

SERVES 4

4tbsp vegetable oil

3 garlic cloves, finely sliced

1kg choi sum or other greens

1 red chilli, finely sliced (deseeded if preferred)

3tbsp oyster sauce

1tbsp light soy sauce

Ideally, you should buy choi sum for this dish, though it also works well with other Chinese greens. This is delicious in its own right, and it is also a brilliant accompaniment for any kind of lightly cooked fish, pork or poultry.

Bring a large pan of water to the boil. Meanwhile, put the oil and garlic in a saucepan and fry the garlic until golden brown. If it becomes too dark, discard and start again as it will taste bitter. Strain the oil into a wok or frying pan, retaining the garlic for later. When the water has come to a vigorous boil, add the greens and after 30 seconds, drain them. Heat the wok over a high heat and add the chilli. Stir-fry for a few seconds, add the greens and stir around. Finally, add the oyster sauce, soy and garlic slices. Make sure everything is well coated before turning into a bowl.

Braised Cherry Tomatoes with Garlic and Lemon

SERVES 4

400g cherry vine tomatoes

75ml white wine

75ml olive oil

75ml water

1tbsp sugar

2 garlic cloves, finely sliced

Grated rind of 1 lemon

2tsp chopped thyme

2 bay leaves, torn into pieces

When most tomatoes are lacking in flavour, you can generally rely on cherry vine tomatoes to be sweet. This is one of the most useful recipes I know – it produces a delicious sauce, which goes well with veal and fish.

Preheat the oven to 220°C/425°F/Gas Mark 7. Destalk the tomatoes or leave them on the vine if you prefer a more rustic look. Place all the ingredients into a roasting tray, large enough to fit everything in snugly. Prick most of the tomatoes with the tip of a sharp knife to help release their juices during cooking. Cover the roasting tray with foil and bake in the oven for at least 30 minutes. What you are aiming for is a deliciously potent sauce made up from the wine, tomato juice, sugar, garlic and lemon. The tomatoes themselves should be cooked but by no means on the point of disintegration. Either serve immediately or leave to cool for later use. As with all tomato-based dishes, its flavour will improve with time, so making it in advance and reheating is the best option.

BASIC RECIPES

Vanilla Ice Cream

½ vanilla pod

300ml double cream

300ml milk

4 egg yolks

120g caster sugar

Scrape the seeds from the vanilla pod using a small sharp knife. Place the seeds, the pod, cream and milk into a pan and carefully bring to the boil. Reduce the heat and simmer for 10 minutes, then set aside for at least 30 minutes. Beat the egg yolks and sugar in a bowl until pale and fluffy. Carefully pour in the milk-cream mixture, whisking all the time. Return this mixture to the pan over the lowest possible heat and gently cook until it thickens. On no account let it boil. The thickening process is difficult to judge, even for professionals. It is essential to stir constantly over a very low heat. The usual advice is to cook the ice cream until it coats the back of a spoon without running, but I am not convinced this is the most reliable test, as this stage can often be reached before the ice cream is ready. Always have a bowl of ice-cold water on stand by into which you can dip the pan should it get too hot. (An ice cream that has curdled slightly can be saved by liquidizing the mix.)

Pass the ice cream through a fine sieve and cool. Pour the mix into your ice cream machine and churn until thickened. Transfer to a freezerproof container and freeze until required.

Chicken Stock

MAKES 2 LITRES

4kg chicken bones, including wings, but not giblets

2 onions, roughly chopped

4 carrots, roughly chopped

2 leek tops, rinsed and roughly chopped

½ head of garlic, unpeeled

½ head of celery, rinsed and roughly chopped

5 black peppercorns

½ bunch of thyme

2 bay leaves

Making fresh stock can be laborious process but, in truth, it's mostly washing up. Stock freezes well, so it's always worth making it in large batches. We reduce our stock by half to concentrate its flavour – if it's too strong, you can always dilute it with water.

Place the chicken bones into a roomy pot and cover with cold water. Bring to the boil and once boiling vigorously, turn down to a simmer. Any resulting scum and fat needs to be skimmed off throughout. After about 30 minutes, the worst will be over and it is time to add the vegetables and herbs. (You could add the vegetables at the beginning but it is easier to skim the stock without them). Bring back to the boil, then reduce the heat and allow to simmer for another 3 hours or so. The next stage is to strain the bones: the best way to do this is to tip all the ingredients into a colander suspended over a large bowl. Give the colander a good shake and dispose of the bones and cooked vegetables. Now pour the stock through a fine sieve or muslin into a clean pan. Put the pan over a high heat and boil the liquid to reduce it by about half. Leave the stock to cool completely and then freeze in suitable containers.

Fish Stock

MAKES 2 LITRES

Vegetable oil

2 onions, finely sliced

2 carrots, finely chopped

2 leek tops, rinsed and finely chopped

½ head of garlic, finely chopped

2 ribs of celery, finely chopped

1 head fennel, trimmed and finely chopped

5 black peppercorns

½ bunch of thyme

5 parsley stalks and leaves

2 bay leaves

4kg fish bones and heads, washed and with the gills removed

350ml white wine

A classic fish stock is made with the bones of expensive flat fish, such as turbot and sole. Purists may scoff but I think the odd salmon head or two can improve things no end. Should you find yourself with any shellfish remains, such as crab, langoustine or prawn shells, smash them up with a rolling pin and freeze until you are ready to make the stock. The magnificent fragrance will remind you that the small fortune originally laid out was money well spent.

Heat a heavy-bottomed pan. Add a scant tablespoon of oil and gently fry the vegetables and herbs for 10 minutes until softened. Add the fish bones, cover and cook for 5 minutes, giving the pan a shake occasionally. You do not want any colour on the fish or vegetables. Add the wine and cover with cold water. Bring to a rapid boil, then reduce the heat and simmer for about 30 minutes, skimming off any unpleasant-looking substances that come to the surface. Stage one is now complete. Place the bones in a colander suspended over a clean pan to catch the drips. Give the colander a shake then discard the vegetables and bones. Strain the stock through a fine sieve or muslin into the washed pan then bring to the boil. Boil rapidly until the liquid is reduced by about half, skimming regularly. Leave to cool completely and then freeze in suitable containers.

Red Wine Gravy

MAKES ABOUT 500ML

Vegetable oil

1 large onion, very finely sliced

1 large carrot, very finely sliced

2 leek tops, rinsed and very
    finely sliced

1 rib of celery, very finely sliced

3 garlic cloves, very finely sliced

1tsp plain flour

350ml red wine

1 bay leaf

1 thyme sprig

1 rosemary sprig

1tsp tomato purée

1tsp redcurrant jelly

500ml reduced Chicken Stock (see
    page 151)

Salt and pepper

If you think you could improve on your normal Sunday roast gravy, this recipe may help and it can be made two or three days in advance. The red wine gives it a lively edge ideal for fatty roasts such as beef and lamb – with the latter, freshly chopped mint is a wonderful addition.

Heat a thin film of oil in a heavy-bottomed, roomy frying pan until the smoking point. Add your vegetables, in 2 stages if necessary, and fry over a high heat until they are well coloured, almost charred in places. Sprinkle over the flour, mix slightly and turn off the heat. Tip the vegetables into a large saucepan and add all the remaining ingredients except the Chicken Stock. Now bring the contents up to the boil, reduce the heat and simmer, stirring from time to time to avoid catching. When the wine has reduced by about three-quarters, stick your finger in and taste. You are looking for something slightly tart. Add the Chicken Stock and boil hard until you have the desired consistency. At this stage, add salt and pepper and leave for a few minutes. Taste again and if you feel the gravy is still too sour, either add more salt or add more redcurrant jelly. If I am being slightly vague here, it is because the quality of the wine and sweetness of the vegetables can be so variable. Once you are satisfied that you have a good-tasting sauce, strain through a fine sieve or muslin and store until needed. It freezes well.

Roast Tomatoes

SERVES 4–6

10 vine tomatoes, destalked, cored
    and cut in half horizontally

2 tbsp extra virgin olive oil

2 garlic cloves, finely chopped

½tsp dried herbes de Provence

Salt and pepper

Tomatoes are so poor for most of the year that it makes sense to try and concentrate their flavour. This recipe involves cooking the tomatoes overnight in a very low oven and then leaving them to cool They can be used for a myriad purposes: in salads, dressings, omelettes, gratins and so on.

Preheat the oven to 90°C. Place the tomatoes on a wire rack on a baking tray. Drizzle over the olive oil, scatter the garlic and herbs and season generously with salt and pepper. If you think the tomatoes are particularly lacking in flavour, try sprinkling a small amount of sugar on them. Bake for at least 8 hours, or longer.

Mayonnaise

MAKES ABOUT 250ML

2 egg yolks

1tsp Dijon mustard

2tbsp white wine vinegar or
    lemon juice

Salt and pepper

250ml vegetable oil

Mayonnaise is easy and shop-bought versions do not compare. Adding the salt at the beginning helps it dissolve more easily.

Mix the first 3 ingredients together with plenty of salt and pepper. Gradually add the oil, initially drop by drop and then in a steady stream. If you find it is curdling or splitting, stop and add a little hot water. Usually this will work. In the event of failure, do not despair. Start again in a clean bowl with 1 more egg yolk and add the curdled mixture gradually. Store in the fridge for up to 2 weeks.

Aïoli

MAKES ABOUT 550ML

2 egg yolks

1tsp Dijon mustard

2tbsp lemon juice or white
    wine vinegar

Salt and pepper

5tbsp water

500ml vegetable oil

2tbsp extra virgin olive oil

2 garlic cloves, crushed to a paste

There is more than one way to make a proper aïoli - I have created a milder and less pungent version that is great with chips.

Put the first 4 ingredients into the bowl of a food processor and season generously. With the motor running, add the vegetable oil – drop by drop to start with then in a steady stream. Keep a watchful eye on the mix as you add the oil. If it starts to curdle, stop and add a tablespoon of boiling water. Add the olive oil and garlic, check the seasoning and add more salt if necessary. Store in the fridge, although this doesn't keep as well as mayonnaise. I would suggest making it no more that a day in advance.

Béchamel Sauce

MAKES ABOUT 500ML

500ml milk

½ onion, finely chopped

1 clove

1 bay leaf

50g butter

50g plain white flour

Salt and pepper

Bring the milk, onion, clove and bay leaf to the boil, then reduce the heat and simmer for 10 minutes. Turn off the heat and leave the milk to infuse for at least 30 minutes. Melt the butter in a roomy, heavy-bottomed pan, then add the flour and cook this mixture over a very low heat for 5 minutes, making sure it does not colour. Pour the hot, strained milk, initially 2 or 3 tablespoons at a time, stirring constantly. As the sauce loosens, you can increase the amount of milk each time. Once all the milk has been added, simmer gently for a few minutes, stirring all the time. Finally season with salt and pepper and if not using immediately, cover with buttered greaseproof paper. Note: you can correct a lumpy sauce by beating it in a blender or liquidizer.

Slow-cooked Tomato Sauce

MAKES 1 LITRE

5tbsp extra virgin olive oil

1 large onion, finely chopped

2 garlic cloves, finely chopped

½ rib of celery, finely chopped

Salt and pepper

1kg canned chopped tomatoes

2tsp dried herbes de Province

1 bay leaf

This recipe produces a rich, herby sauce ideal for vegetable lasagnes and other pasta dishes. It freezes well and improves if made a day in advance.

Heat the olive oil in a large heavy-bottomed saucepan. When hot, add the vegetables and a liberal dose of salt and pepper. Turn the heat down to low and gently cook the vegetables for at least 30 minutes without colouring them. By necessity, this means keeping a careful eye on the pan, stirring from time to time. The idea is to bring out the maximum amount of sweetness to counteract the acidity of the tomatoes. Add the tomatoes and herbs, bring back to the boil, then reduce the heat and simmer for another 90 minutes, stirring at least every 5 minutes. Adjust the seasoning with extra salt and pepper.

Vinaigrette

MAKES 300ML

50ml good-quality red wine vinegar

2tsp Dijon mustard

2tsp sugar

Salt and pepper

250ml vegetable oil

1 thyme sprig

2 garlic cloves, lightly crushed

This is a good general dressing. You can adjust it by adding more sugar, mustard or garlic. As a general rule, however, you should be aiming for a ratio of one part vinegar to four or five parts oil. A good tip is to add the salt and sugar to the vinegar at the outset and leave it to dissolve for at least 5 minutes before you add any oil.

Mix the vinegar, mustard and sugar with salt and pepper and leave to dissolve for 5 minutes. Gradually add the oil in a steady stream until you have a semi-emulsified liquid. Add the thyme and garlic and refrigerate in a screwtop jar until needed. Give the jar a good shake before using.

Apple and Horseradish Sauce

MAKES 8-10

3 large Bramley cooking apples

4½tbsp caster sugar

90ml water

3 cloves

Juice of ¾ lemon

180g fresh horseradish, peeled and finely grated

Viennese in origin, it is traditionally served with veal. It is delicious with roast pork too.

Peel the apples and cut into chunks. Place the apples and the other ingredients, except the horseradish, into a pan. Bring to the boil, then reduce the heat and simmer over a very low heat for about 40 minutes. Be vigilant and stir every 5 minutes. Remove the pan from the heat and stir in the horseradish. Put aside to cool.

Bread Sauce

225ml milk
½ onion, finely chopped
4 cloves
½ bay leaf
½ thyme sprig
55g fresh breadcrumbs
40g butter, plus extra for greasing
Salt and pepper
2tbsp double cream

To make the bread sauce, place the milk, onion, cloves, bay leaf and thyme into a small saucepan and bring to the boil. Reduce the heat and simmer for 15 minutes, stirring occasionally to stop the milk from catching. Put aside the milk to infuse, ideally for at least an hour. Strain the milk into a clean pan and bring back to the boil. Turn off the heat and stir in the breadcrumbs and butter, then season with salt and pepper. Pour in the double cream, cover with some buttered paper and leave to rest in a warm place.

Sweet Pastry

500g plain white flour
240g butter
100g sugar
Pinch of salt
2 egg yolks, beaten
100ml iced water

This makes enough pastry to line two 23-cm tart rings. As with all pastry, it freezes well and can be kept for later use.

In an electric mixer, beat the flour, butter, sugar and salt together until they resemble coarse breadcrumbs with no traces of butter visible. Add the egg yolks and water and beat until the mass starts to come together. At this stage, remove the pastry and kneed into a smooth ball. Divide the pastry into 2 portions and wrap both in clingfilm. Refrigerate for at least 30 minutes before rolling out. You can freeze the second ball if not required for immediate use.

Savoury Pastry

600g plain white flour
300g butter
Salt and pepper
140ml iced cold water

This produces enough pastry to line two 28-cm tart rings or three 23-cm tart rings. Pastry freezes well so it is worth making more than your immediate needs.

In an electric mixer, beat the flour and butter together until they resemble coarse breadcrumbs with no lumps of butter visible. Add a little salt and pepper and then add the water which should be as cold as possible. Once the pastry starts to come together, stop the beating and turn out onto a work surface. Quickly kneed the crumbly mass into a smooth ball. Divide the pastry equally into 2 or 3 portions, depending on the size of your tart ring. Wrap each portion in clingfilm and rest in the fridge for at least 30 minutes before use. Freeze the remainder for later use.

RECOMMENDED SUPPLIERS

The internet and mail order represents the best hope for the honest, small producer up against the mighty supermarket chains. Almost all of the suppliers listed will despatch by overnight delivery to anywhere within the United Kingdom.

MEAT

Border County Foods

Their sausages contain nothing but free-range rare-breed pork and seasonings. Their black pudding is made from fresh English pig's blood.

The Old Vicarage
Crosby-on-Eden
Cumbria CA6 4QZ
01228 573500
www.cumberland-sausage.net

Ellel Free Range Poultry Company

Small producers of traditionally reared birds, including guinea fowl, geese, bronze turkeys and Poulet de Bresse chickens.

The Stables
Ellel Grange
Galgate Nr Lancaster,
Lancashire LA2 0HN
01524 751200
www.ellelfreerangepoultry.co.uk

Graig Farm Organics

This award-winning enterprise works with a group of farmers across Wales to offer a vast range of organic or free-range meats and other products.

Dolau
Lllandrindod wells
Powys LD1 5TL
01597 851655
www.graigfarm.co.uk

Happy Meats

Happy Meat's rare-breed pigs are raised in small family groups on an additive- and GM-free diet. Also grass-fed, rare breed beef and lamb, venison and other game.

Happy Meats Limited
Bank House Farm
Stanford Bridge
Worcestershire WR6 6RU
01886 812 485
www.happymeats.co.uk

Pentre Pigs

A small, enthusiastic producer of traditional free-range Berkshire, Tamworth and Kune Kune pigs.

Pentre House
LeightonWelshpool
Powys SY21 8HL
01938 553430
www.pentrepigs.co.uk

Sheepdrove Organic Farm

This organic, mixed farm produces well-hung beef from South Devon and Aberdeen Angus suckler herds plus lamb, mutton, pork and slow-grown chickens. Useful small items include lardons, chicken "stockpot bags" and pots of organic chicken livers.

Warren Farm,
Lambourn,
Berkshire RG17 7UU
01488 71659
www.sheepdrove.com

The Real Meat Company

The Real Meat company has a strict code of welfare standards, which result in fine meat.

The Real Meat Company
Warminster BA12 0HR
0845 7626017
www.realmeat.co.uk

Wild Meat Company

Low Road, Sweffling,
Saxmundham,
Suffolk IP17 2BU
01728 663221
www.wildmeat.co.uk

FISH

Severn and Wye Smokery

Fabulous smoked salmon and other products using traditional methods.

Chaxhill
Westbury on Severn
Gloucestershire GL14 1QW

01452 760190
www.severnandwye.co.uk
London agent: Lorna Heaton,
lorheaton@aol.com, 020 7603 0471

Cornish Fish Direct
Fresh fish caught from Cornish boats using environmentally friendly fishing methods.

The Pilchard Works
Newlyn
Penzance Cornwall
01736 332 112
www.cornishfish.com

Keltic Seafare (Scotland) Ltd
For fabulous scallops, langoustines and other shellfish. Also wonderful wild mushrooms when in season.

Unit 6, Strathpeffer Road
Industrial Estate
Dingwall
Ross-shire IV15 9SP
01349 864087
www.kelticseafare.com

Loch Fyne Oysters
Offers a lot more than just oysters – fresh and smoked salmon, shellfish, mussels and herrings.

Clachan
Cairndow
Argyll PA26 8BL
01499 600264
www.loch-fyne.com

VEGETABLES

Martin Pitt Freedom Eggs

Great House Farm
Gwehelog
Near Usk
Monmouthshire NP15 1RJ
01291 673129
www.freedomeggs.co.uk

Mrs Tee's Wild Mushrooms

Gorse Meadow
Sway Road
Lymington,
Hampshire SO41 8LR
01590 673354
www.wildmushrooms.co.uk

Riverford Farm
Riverford Farm in Devon grows over 80 varieties of organic vegetables and fruit and also produces its own cream and milk.

Wash Barn
Buckfastleigh
Devon TQ11 0LD
0845 600 2311
www.riverford.co.uk

Andreas Georghiou
Friendly and helpful – delivery service throughout west London.

Andreas Georghiou & Co.
35 Turnham Green Terrace
Chiswick, W4 1RG
020 8995 0140
www.andreasveg.co.uk

EQUIPMENT

Divertimenti
London shops selling quality cookware.

227–229 Brompton Road
London SW3 2EP
020 7581 8065
www.divertimenti.co.uk

Dorset Charcoal Company
Supplies barbecue charcoal from sustainable sources.

Tudor Cottage
Pidney
Hazelbury Bryan
Dorset DT10 2EB
01258 818176
www.dorsetcharcoal.co.uk

Nisbets
Mail order suppliers of professional catering equipment – everything from mandolins to moulis at a reasonable price.

1110 Aztec West
Bristol
BS32 4HR
0845 1405555
www.nisbets.co.uk

Mobile knife-sharpening service for London
Will come to your door. Let the neighbours know and get those knives out!

David Baggia 0208 8567967

INDEX

aïoli 153
apple(s)
    and horseradish sauce 154
    Norfolk apple and treacle tart 137
apricots: carrot cake with apricots and
    lemon fromage frais 139
artichokes
    Jerusalem artichoke gratin 149
    salad of monkfish and baby 43
asparagus,
    feta and spiced couscous salad 26
avocados
    salad of Cos lettuce, avocado and
        Parmesan dressing 28
    smoked salmon, flour tortillas,
        avocado salsa, soured cream and
        lime 106

bacon
    chicken and bacon pie 116
    sandwich of bacon, dolcelatte, baby
        spinach, tomato and roast red
        onion 110
baked gurnard wrapped in Parma ham
    with red pepper, fennel and olives
    119
baking blind 12
bananas: toasted banana bread with
    butterscotch sauce 136
béchamel sauce 153
beef
    grilled bavette steak with tomato
        and tarragon butter 58
    and kidney casserole with creamed
        horseradish 129
    Mussaman curry with toasted
        peanuts 62
beer-battered skate cheeks with pickled
    onion and parsley mayonnaise 40
beetroot
    and celeriac, cep and bacon soup 90
    sea trout with beetroot, bacon,
        sorrel and horseradish 48
black bean chilli with coriander and
    soured cream 128
blood orange and mint jelly 143
boil 11
boulangere potatoes 148
braised cherry tomatoes with garlic
    and lemon 150
bread sauce 155
broad bean, asparagus, feta and spiced
    couscous salad 26
broccoli: steamed purple sprouting
    broccoli with red chilli and anchovy
    dressing 100

brown sugar meringue with
    strawberries and oranges 74
butternut and goat's cheese lasagne
    123

calf's liver with creamed lentils,
    mustard and bacon 125
carrot cake with apricots and lemon
    fromage frais 139
cauliflower: aubergine, sweet potato
    and cauliflower curry 70
celery 13
chargrilled squid, chickpea purée,
    roasted pepper and lemon salsa 44
cheesecake: chocolate and
    mascarpone 140
cherry and almond tart 76
chicken
    and bacon pie 116
    Goan chicken curry with roasted
        coconut and fresh onion chutney
        66
    and Parma ham terrine 36
    pot-roast chicken with leeks and
        anchovies 120
    salad of poached chicken, green
        beans, watercress, capers and
        mayonnaise 29
    smoked chicken and sweetcorn
        broth 87
    spatchcocked chicken marinated
        with yoghurt 60
    stock 151
    Vietnamese chicken patties with
        lime dipping sauce 42
chickpeas
    chargrilled squid, chickpea purée,
        roasted pepper and lemon salsa
        44
    spiced chickpea fritters with sesame
        dressing 24
    spiced sweet potato and chickpea
        soup 88
chillies: black bean chilli with
    coriander and soured cream 128
chips 147
chocolate
    and hazelnut terrine 77
    honeycomb crisp ice cream with
        warm chocolate sauce 73
    and mascarpone cheesecake 140
chop 12
clams 15
spaghetti with clams, smoked bacon
    and garlic 38
cockles 15
cod: deep-fried salt cod fritters with
    piquillo peppers, green bean and
    rocket salad 98
conversion tables 11, 12
crab, tomato and saffron tart 35

cream tart with stewed rhubarb and
    orange 144
creamed leeks and mint 148
curried smoked haddock and lentil soup
    89
curries
    aubergine, sweet potato and
        cauliflower 70
    Goan chicken curry with roasted
        coconut and fresh onion chutney
        66
    hot-and-sour pork curry with raita
        63
    lamb, fig and mint tagine 69
    Mussaman beef curry with toasted
        peanuts 62
    Thai yellow fish curry with tiger
        prawns and scallops 64

deep-fried salt cod fritters with piquillo
    peppers, green bean and rocket
    salad 98
dry-roasting 12

equipment, kitchen 18-19

fish
    cooking tips 13
    portion sizes 11
    stock 151

gammon, molasses-glazed 131
garlic 13
grated 12
gnocchi: potato gnocchi with tomato
    sauce, mascarpone and mint 115
Goan chicken curry with roasted
    coconut and fresh onion chutney 66
gravy, red wine 152
green vegetables 13
griddled scallops with spiced red
    lentils 47
grilled bavette steak with tomato and
    tarragon butter 58
gurnard: baked gurnard wrapped in
    Parma ham 119

haddock
    curried haddock and lentil soup 89
    omelette of smoked haddock 109
    smoked haddock gratin 114
ham: yellow split pea and ham soup 94
herbs 14
herring: warm salad of smoked
    herring, new potatoes, shallots and
    mustard 104
honeycomb crisp ice cream with warm
    chocolate sauce 73

jelly: blood orange and mint 143
Jerusalem artichoke gratin 149

kale: curly kale, potato and chorizo soup 93

lamb
    and aubergine and red onion kebab with pilaff rice 57
    and fig and mint tagine 69
    koftas with tomato, onion and coriander relish 67
    with potatoes, pearl barley, red pepper and sherry 133
lasagne: butternut and goat's cheese 123
linguini with squid, chilli and lemon 32
liver: calf's liver with creamed lentils, mustard and bacon 125

mackerel: mackerel with paprika 51
mashed potato 147
mayonnaise 153
meringue: brown sugar meringue with strawberries and oranges 74
monkfish: warm salad of grilled monkfish and baby artichokes 43
Mussaman beef curry with peanuts 62
mussels 15
    steamed mussels with cider, 31

Norfolk apple and treacle tart 137

omelette of smoked haddock, spring onion, potato, Parmesan 109
onions 14
    sweet onion and Parmesan tart 23
    white onion and cider soup 85

pappardelle with winter greens, fontina, onions, cherry tomatoes and pecorino 103
partridge: roast partridge, Savoy cabbage and bread sauce 126
pastry
    savoury 155
    sweet 155
peaches and cream 79
pears: upside-down pear and ginger cake 135
pepper 14
peppers, roast 14
pig's cheeks braised with red wine, button onions, mushrooms and bacon 124
plums: twice-cooked belly of pork with homemade plum sauce 52
poach 12
pork
    hot-and-sour pork curry with raita 63
    slow-roast belly of pork, 132
    treacle-marinated pork chops 55
    twice-cooked belly of pork 52

pot-roast chicken with leeks and anchovies 120
potato(es)
    aubergine, sweet potato and cauliflower curry 70
    boulangere 148
    chips 147
    curly kale, potato and chorizo soup 93
    gnocchi with slow-cooked tomato sauce, mascarpone and mint 115
    mashed 147
    roasted butternut and sweet potato wedges 99
    spiced sweet potato and chickpea soup 88
    spring onion, potato and Taleggio risotto 112
    tortilla with chorizo in red wine 25
prawns
    sandwich of prawns, curried mayonnaise and baby Gem 37
    Thai yellow fish curry with tiger prawns and scallops 64
pulses 13

raita 63
raspberry flapjack and vanilla ice cream sundae 80
rhubarb: cream tart with stewed rhubarb and orange 144
risotto: spring onion, potato and Taleggio 112
roast partridge: Savoy cabbage and bread sauce 126
roast peppers 14
roast tomatoes 14, 152
roasted butternut and sweet potato wedges, chilli sauce and sour cream 99
roasts 14

sardines: grilled sardines with marinated fennel and lemon salad 54
sausages: spagetti with Italian sausage, mushrooms and red chilli 108
scallops
    griddled scallops with red lentils 47
    Thai yellow fish curry with prawns 65
sea trout with beetroot, bacon, sorrel and horseradish 48
seasoning 10
shellfish 15
simmer 12
skate: beer-battered skate cheeks with pickled onion and mayonnaise 40
slow-roast belly of pork, red cabbage, apple and horseradish sauce 132
smoked chicken and sweetcorn broth 87

smoked haddock gratin with potato, tomato, spinach, crème fraîche and Gruyère 114
smoked salmon, flour tortillas, avocado, salsa, soured cream and lime 106
spatchcocked chicken marinated with yoghurt 60
spiced chickpea fritters with sesame dressing 24
spiced sweet potato and chickpea soup 88
spices 15
spring onion, potato and Taleggio risotto 112
squid
    chargrilled squid 44
    linguini with squid, chilli & lemon 32
steamed greens, red chill, oyster sauce and garlic 149
steamed mussels with cider, crème fraîche and thyme 31
steamed purple sprouting broccoli with red chilli and anchovy dressing 100
stocks 10
    chicken 151
    fish 151
sweet onion and Parmesan tart 23

Thai yellow fish curry wit tiger prawns and scallops 64
toasted banana bread with butterscotch sauce 136
tomato(es)
    braised cherry tomatoes with garlic and lemon 150
    roast 14, 152
    sauce 154
treacle-marinated pork chops with apple and celeriac salad 55

upside-down pear and ginger cake 135

vanilla ice cream 150
Vietnamese chicken patties with lime dipping sauce 42
vinaigrette 154

warm salad of grilled monkfish and baby artichokes 43
warm salad of smoked herring, new potatoes, shallots and mustard 104
white onion and cider soup 85
winter salad of roast parsnips, green beans, lentils, poached egg and curried dressing 97

yellow split pea and ham soup 94

Acknowledgements

There are so many people I would like to thank.

My mum, Liz, for her love and support and for inspiring me to cook in the first place! Michael Halden for his immense kindness in introducing me to Pavilion Books and with Loma, for their unflagging and generous encouragement throughout. I would particularly like to thank Marcus Leaver for commissioning the book and for his ongoing support – without him, the book would never have happened. Peter Richnell, my business partner, whose judicious and friendly nature have led to ten years of really good fun and a vibrant, convivial environment. Myles Nelson, for his fabulous photography and Aussie grace under pressure (mylonelson@hotmail.com). And not least, my current kitchen team – Al Volev, Sholto Gouk, Poogie, Acland Geddes, Roger Rahaman – a multi-talented and inspirational bunch who have given me the time and space to write the book.

I would also like to thank the many chefs who I have had the pleasure of working with over the years. I'd like to name them all but I feel I must mention Carole Craddock, Kylie Hobson, Krissy Garvan, Lia Lawlor, Zoltan and Tako Jabang – collectively and individually, they have all played a huge part in building The Havelock's reputation and keeping the show on the road. I would particularly like to thank the prodigiously gifted Joanne Wilkinson and Jim Garvan, both of whom taught me so much and were instrumental in establishing our initial success. I'd also like to thank Mark Robinson, the most thoughtful and adventurous of cooks, who runs our sister pub, The Earl Spencer, in south-west London. Finally, I'd like to pay tribute to Christophe, who has been entertaining us all with his charm and "Manuel-like" behaviour for what seems like an eternity.

At Pavilion Books, I'd like to thank the entire team: Lizzy Gray who has so ably led the project and whose incisive and relaxed approach has made the whole process seem very smooth; Kate Oldfield for her sparkly support and for backing the book from the off; Adelle Morris and Gemma Wilson for the excellent page design. Thanks also to Beverly LeBlanc for her encouragement and extremely tight recipe editing.

Last but by no means least, I really do owe everything to Camilla – with Georgia, Gus and Max, I hope we continue to have many more years of culinary bliss!